Liberal Democrats Do God

Edited by Jo Latham and Claire Mathys

Liberal Democrats Do God

Edited by Jo Latham and Claire Mathys

Liberal Democrat
Christian Forum

First published in Great Britain in 2013

Liberal Democrat Christian Forum
Level 2, 8-10 Great George Street
London SW1P 3AE
Email: office@ldcf.net
Website: www.ldcf.net

Photo of Paul Tyler © Paul Heartfield
Typeset in Baskerville

Designed by www.natgillet.co.uk

Contents

About the Contributors

Steve Webb MP

Steve Webb is MP for Thornbury and Yate and the Minister of State for Pensions. He has previously been Liberal Democrat spokesman for a number of portfolios including Work and Pensions, Energy and Climate Change, and Health. Before his election to Parliament in 1997, Steve worked for the Institute for Fiscal Studies and as Professor of Social Policy at Bath University. He lives in his constituency with his wife Helen, their two teenage children and Sally the dog.

John Pugh MP

John Pugh was elected as the Member of Parliament for Southport in 2001. He is the Co-Chair of the Party's Parliamentary Committee for Health and Social Care. Born in Liverpool in 1948, John went on to study philosophy at Durham University and subsequently became a teacher. His interests include the study of philosophy, logic, mental health, and education. He and his wife, Annette, have three daughters and a son.

Tim Farron MP

Tim Farron became MP for Westmorland and Lonsdale in 2005, winning by 267 votes. In 2010 he achieved an 11.1% swing from the Conservatives to increase his majority to over 12,000. Tim has been Parliamentary Private Secretary to former party leader Sir Menzies Campbell and was later promoted to Shadow Defra Secretary. In 2010 he was elected President of the Liberal Democrats.

Greg Mulholland MP

Greg Mulholland is the Liberal Democrat MP for Leeds North West. A former Leeds City Councillor, Greg was first elected to Parliament in 2005. He was then re-elected in 2010. Greg studied politics at the University of York before his successful career in marketing. He now lives with his wife Raegan and their three young daughters in Otley.

Rt Hon Sir Andrew Stunell MP

Andrew Stunell has been the Liberal Democrat MP for Hazel Grove since 1997. He was Parliamentary Under-Secretary of State in the Department for Communities and Local Government from May 2010-September 2012 and was a member of the Liberal Democrat negotiating team which led to the formation of the Coalition. Amongst others, Andrew has strong interests in third world issues, sustainability and energy policy. He is married to Gillian and they have five grown up children. They are active members of Romiley Methodist Church.

Rt Hon Sir Alan Beith MP

Alan Beith was elected as MP for Berwick-upon-Tweed in a by-election in 1973 and has held the seat ever since. He is a former Chief Whip and former Deputy Leader of the Liberal Party and then the Liberal Democrats. He is currently Chair of the Justice and Liaison Select Committees, Chairman of the Historic Chapels Trust, and a Methodist lay preacher.

Lord Tyler

Paul Tyler became a County Councillor at 22; a Liberal MP at 32; a Liberal Democrat MP at 52; and then Chief Whip. He is now a Peer who still campaigns for democratic reform of the House of Lords at 72. Paul also chairs the Faiths and Civil Society Unit at Goldsmiths, University of London.

Lord Roberts of Llandudno

Roger Roberts was born in October 1935 and educated at John Bright Grammar School Llandudno, University College of North Wales and Handsworth Methodist College Birmingham. A Methodist Minister since 1957, Rev. Roberts was Superintendent for 20 years, now serving as a Supernumerary. He was a long-serving President of the Welsh Liberals/Liberal Democrats. He is a former Leader of the Liberal Democrats on Aberconwy Council and was candidate for Conwy constituency five times. He is a widower with three children and lives in Llandudno.

Baroness Brinton

Sal Brinton wrote her first letter to a political prisoner when she was eight years old. This was the start of many years of political activism. She entered the House of Lords as a peer in 2011 where her main interest is education. Sal is also passionate about ensuring that those who flee from persecution find asylum. She and her husband Tim live and worship in Watford, where Tim chairs the Watford and Three Rivers Refugee Project.

Mark Williams MP

Mark Williams is the Welsh Liberal Democrat MP for Ceredigion. He was born in 1966 and attended Aberystwyth University, graduating in 1987. Formerly a Deputy Headteacher near Brecon, he was elected as the MP for Ceredigion in 2005 with a majority of just 219 votes. In 2010 he was re-elected with an increased majority of 8,324 votes taking 50% of the vote. He lives with his wife Helen in Borth, with their three young daughters Eleanor, Anna and Eliza and their son Oliver.

Duncan Hames MP

Duncan Hames has been the Member of Parliament for Chippenham since May 2010 and the Parliamentary Private Secretary to Nick Clegg since 2012. In addition to his responsibilities as a constituency MP, Duncan takes an active interest in renewable energy and low carbon technologies, previously working as an aide to Energy Secretaries Ed Davey and Chris Huhne.

Sarah Teather MP

Sarah Teather is the MP for Brent Central. She was elected to Parliament in a by-election in 2003 to become the youngest MP in Parliament. She served for two and a half years as the Minister of State for Children and Families in the Department for Education and is now a backbencher and Chair of the All Party Parliamentary Group on Refugees.

About the Liberal Democrat Christian Forum

The Liberal Democrat Christian Forum (LDCF) exists to be a Christian voice in the Liberal Democrat Party, and a voice of liberal democracy among Christians. It seeks to support Christians of all backgrounds in their constructive work in politics.

LDCF is an Associated Organisation of the Liberal Democrat Party, and consist of party members, Councillors, MPs, and Peers, as well as Christians who are not members of the Liberal Democrat Party but who are sympathetic towards its values and wish to support the ministry of LDCF.

LDCF has existed since the birth of the Liberal Democrat Party in 1988 and has four main aims:

1. To support and encourage Christians within the party, helping them to live out their faith through politics at national, regional and local levels

2. To act as a bridge between the Christian community and the party, building relationships with Christian organisations, charities, churches and the media

3. To encourage Christians to become more politically engaged – to see politics as mission and a way of seeking justice for their community and nation

4. To underpin all that it does with prayer, and to pray regularly for the government and nation

If you would like to support LDCF in this vision, or to receive support from LDCF as a Christian in the party, please join at www.ldcf.net/join or request more information by sending an email to office@ldcf.net or visiting our website: www.ldcf.net.

Acknowledgements

We would like to thank John Pugh MP for providing the inspiration for this publication and general oversight; Joanna Hobson for her editorial assistance; and Nat Gillet for his design work.

Introduction

Steve Webb MP
MP for Thornbury & Yate and Minister of State for Pensions

One of the most remarkable things about this collection of articles is that it exists at all!

Not many years ago, the Liberal Democrat Christian Forum (LDCF) was a small and largely invisible organisation within the party, kept going by the faithful few. But in recent years the group has been transformed, with a growing membership, as a space where Christians within the party from diverse traditions can come together to discuss issues of mutual concern.

This collection of essays confirms that Christians in the Liberal Democrats are a diverse bunch! The LDCF is not a faction out to promote a single Christian agenda within party policy. Rather it is a community which offers support and encouragement to Christians within the party and – crucially – a Liberal Democrat voice into the Christian world. For too long those attending big Christian festivals and expressing an interest in political engagement have found only Labour and Conservative colleagues to talk to. We have been gradually changing that so that politically engaged Christians can see that there is a home for them in the Liberal Democrats.

The most fundamental reason why Christians should feel at home in the Liberal Democrats is that the character of God, as revealed in the Christian Gospel, would suggest that God must be a liberal!

This assertion will shock or offend some, but I believe that there is no other conclusion that can be drawn from a reading of the New Testament.

The Gospel makes it clear that human beings have freedom. Jesus makes it clear that God does not seek slaves, but sons and daughters. And God gave us the most extraordinary freedom – the freedom to reject and crucify his Son. There must be something very precious about freedom, a value dear to the heart of every liberal.

You can only have a relationship with people who willingly and freely relate to you, not with those who are coerced into doing so. If the Almighty Creator of the universe does not impose his will on his creation, then we flawed individuals who are involved in the political process should be deeply cautious of using the power of the state to impose our will on others. Clearly there have to be frameworks and boundaries, and the state is right to impose those. But beyond this, our faith surely teaches us that we should be very wary of anything more coercive. Those who recognise in the Gospel a deep reverence for human freedom and self-determination will find a natural home in the Liberal Democrats.

The chapters which follow provide a mixture of philosophical reflections on the underpinnings of liberalism and some very hands-on, practical examples of how Christianity makes a real difference to the lives of those most in need.

In his opening chapter, John Pugh MP highlights the importance of Christianity to Liberalism: as a foundation for the concept of human rights, an imperative to tackle poverty, and a positive mandate for the state to ensure that markets do not let down the most vulnerable.

Following on from this, party president Tim Farron MP sets out the case for the historical truth of the Christian Gospel and the need for a response. He stresses that being a Christian does not mean promoting 'right wing moral authoritarianism', but does provide an imperative to be 'strident' in speaking out against injustice.

Greg Mulholland MP takes the collection in a new direction, reflecting on his own experiences of religious discrimination at the last General Election and warns the party against intolerance of those within its own ranks whose faith leads them to a view at odds with that of the 'party line'.

In his chapter, Andrew Stunell MP points out the ways in which the church over the years has got things wrong. He believes that modern attitudes to the rights of women and of minority groups reflect a progressive revelation by God of the way in which we should treat each other. He also celebrates the pluralist and secular society in which we live, which should provide us with the space to worship and live according to our beliefs and consciences.

Senior MP Alan Beith, who chairs Parliament's Justice Select Committee, tackles the thorny issue of Crime and Punishment from a liberal and Christian perspective. Whilst recognising that imprisonment will always have a role to play in the criminal justice system, not least to protect society from those who are a danger to it, he argues that the approach of 'restorative justice' offers a more fruitful direction in most cases. He stresses that this is certainly not a 'soft' option, but rather offers a way forward that is more in keeping with a Christian understanding of forgiveness as well as being more effective in practice.

Lord Paul Tyler considers the relationship between Church and state, with particular reference to the Establishment of the Church of England. He highlights the issues raised by the preferential status accorded to the Church of England in the House of Lords, with reserved places for Bishops who still can only be male. He believes that the time may have come to break this link, to the potential benefit of both Church and State. He also stresses the crucial point of a need for 'religious literacy' within both local and central government, especially with the growing role for voluntary sector groups in providing public services.

Lib Dem peers Roger Roberts and Sal Brinton highlight the very practical steps which Christians can take to meet the needs of the vulnerable. In Roger's case this includes action to tackle street homelessness in London, whilst Sal highlights the support given by churches in Watford to those who have fled to the UK seeking sanctuary from their home country. She stresses the repeated Biblical injunction to do justice to those who 'sojourn' in your country.

In a similar vein, Ceredigion MP Mark Williams emphasises the importance of the UK delivering its commitment to a 0.7% of National Income target for aid spending, and recounts the practical difference that such funding is making in Nigeria. He stresses the Liberal Democrat view that education is a fundamental route to human flourishing and welcomes the way that UK aid spending is ensuring that boys and girls in Nigeria get a better education.

Chippenham MP Duncan Hames reflects on the links between Christianity, Liberal Democracy and the environment, explaining why these should be natural bedfellows. As the 'Greenest' of the major political parties, many Liberal Democrats are committed environmentalists, and Duncan highlights the way in which these issues have risen up the agenda of many Christian churches and Christian environmental groups.

Finally, Sarah Teather, MP for the inner London constituency of Brent Central, makes a powerful plea for Christian language and engagement on the thorny issues of welfare reform and immigration. She highlights the demonisation of benefit recipients and immigrants in the popular press and in the speeches of many politicians and urges our party to stand against this rhetoric rather than go with the flow.

This is a collection which highlights the fact that Christianity is alive and kicking within the Liberal Democrats. Christianity within the party is not a uniform policy package or platform but a diverse and vibrant strand of thinking and practice. Whether you are a Christian who is interested in politics or a Liberal Democrat who is seeking an insight into Christian thinking, I commend this collection to you and echo Tim Farron's invitation to you to join us in this shared endeavour!

Part One:
Why should we 'do God'?

1
'Doing God' in the Liberal Democrat Party

John Pugh MP
MP for Southport

Alastair Campbell famously said of the Blair administration, "We don't do God". His political antennae were telling him that fencing off, or quarantining, religious questions was the safest political strategy. After all, experience from across the Atlantic and indeed in Europe has shown that nailing religious colours firmly to the mast can often be a sure way of polarising people and reducing a party's political appeal and base.

Liberalism in Europe in the past did not usually stop at 'not doing God', but was often expressly anti-clerical, wanting religious institutions to have less power and influence and content to legislate in a manner wholly indifferent to religious sensitivities.

English liberalism, however, has always been a little different; often historically rooted in Methodism, non-conformity and faith-based social reform. Being anti-establishment and tolerant of the outsider meant it could comfortably house within it those of passionate faith and those who passionately rejected all religion. That is still probably the case.

A recent survey of Liberal Democrat membership by Chief Executive Tim Gordon has shown that a surprisingly high percentage of members are affiliated to churches and yet there is a very active, campaigning secular wing. Major donors range from Paul Marshall (Catholic) to Richard Dawkins (Militant Atheist). Equally stark differences have always been found at every level of party representation, and those differences explored – and hitherto usually expressed – without acrimony.

However, in recent years specifically Christian input has been both muted and defensive. Old battles over religious schools and religious education in schools have emerged, evoking the mood of the 'Rome on the Rates!' debates of the previous century (when a cry went up denouncing the public funding of Catholic schools). On sensitive life issues like Euthanasia the Lib Dems uniquely claim a firm, party political position.

There are sometimes, too, some understandable but not well understood differences on how equality legislation should be applied, which have the potential to erupt in an incendiary and painful fashion. Bigotry can be shown both towards and by religion.

In this context it can be questioned whether religious belief is compatible with true Liberalism and vice versa. Worse still, the religious (membership) could be seen as an odd sometime-affiliate of the true Liberal faith, whose strange scruples (conscience) can at best be indulged – but only when it doesn't matter much. It is as though the presence of the religious in the party is a matter of fortuitous accident and has little to do with them actually being religious.

Either outcome – whether a fierce rejection of the Christian world-view or an insincere humouring of it – weakens Liberalism. However much it might gratify its secular wing, there will always be pinch points between religious and party orthodoxy. What will be lost is the significant input Christianity (and other faiths) give to Liberal thinking.

There is of course no straight 'read across' from Christianity to the political policies of any one party, which is why you find Christians in most political parties. The translation of core beliefs into a political programme, we can agree, is a complex matter.

There are, however, areas where Christianity both provides a rationale and an impetus for key Liberal positions. Three crucial and related areas in particular come to mind – human rights, poverty and the role of markets and the state. All I can do here is briefly outline where the merging of Liberalism and Christianity takes us; each deserves a chapter to itself.

Human Rights

The Christian faith makes the extraordinary claim that we are, with our varying physical, mental and moral features, all children of God, made in his image (Imago Dei) and to be valued for that reason. We all have an unquestionable right to flourish, to fulfil that nature and no government or group of individuals should frustrate it.

There is a debate to be had as to whether this extraordinary status is gained at conception, gestation or birth, but there is no doubt it implies that no-one's interest can be ignored or seen as inherently insignificant. As the Gospel largely testifies, a person's value is wholly unrelated to their social status and worldly achievement.

It is far from obvious that someone who believes we are simply the accidental creation of Darwinian evolution in a godless world need believe any of this. It is still perfectly legitimate and generous from an entirely secular viewpoint to claim a catalogue of 'human rights' for one's fellow beings. However, it remains just that; a catalogue – gainsaid and misinterpreted by repressive regimes the world over or lampooned in right wing media when various basic human rights seem to conflict. Victims and criminals for example have human rights but unless they are understood within a wider view of what human beings are about, balancing them without affronting 'common sense' has proved tricky.

The problem is that most talk of 'human rights' began with the religious distinction between the law of God (or natural law) and the law of man (or state law), with the assumption that the latter should be judged against the former. Cut loose from that, intellectual heritage talk about 'human rights' has the tendency to degenerate into shopping lists of conflicting entitlements.

Poverty

Liberals to a man and woman bemoan the unfairness of wealth distribution in our country and indeed in the world. However for some it is not the width of the gap between the rich and the poor that alarms, but the contingent and fortuitous nature of it. In speech after speech Liberals point out the varying outcomes for a child born in central

Birth determines outcomes and the one thing we can't be blamed for is our birth

Manchester as opposed to Maidenhead, or according to where along the Jubilee line they spent their infancy. Birth determines outcomes and the one thing we can't be blamed for is our birth.

However, Liberals classically divide into two groups: those reconciled to appreciable wealth inequality but annoyed that everyone doesn't get the same chance to be rich; and those who, even if everyone had the same chance to get rich, remain unhappy about the wide distribution of wealth – the extremes of wealth and poverty.

'Orange Book' Liberals for example fret more about inequality of opportunity than inequality of outcome (as long as the race is fair the distribution of prizes is not an issue).

Christian Liberals of whatever hue have traditionally seen 'wealth' itself as morally problematic – the parable of Dives and Lazarus, the eye of the needle proverb etc. Christians are taught to be sceptical and indeed humble about any clear link between worldly achievement and genuine personal merit.

This isn't a simple matter and it doesn't necessarily follow that Christian Liberals would favour higher tax rates for the wealthy rather than the encouragement of philanthropy, or disown utterly any concept of 'undeserving poor'. It does mean though that Christians in the Liberal Democrat Party enter the debate on tax and welfare from a particular and distinctive angle.

The State and Markets

This brings us to the role of the state. Liberals and Christians have always been wary of the overweening state but for slightly different reasons. Liberals, because they see it as a threat to individuality and diversity; Christians, because they think it lacks the capacity to ensure that human beings lead a truly happy and fulfilling life. Both see sense in limiting the power of the state – usually as a way of removing the most obvious barriers to happiness and/or self-expression.

Christians who are Liberals, however, are more likely to endorse the view that the state should own or offer some clear vision or concept of the 'common good', whereas agnostic Liberals are more likely to think the state should act as ringmaster leaving individuals to do their own thing.

A concept of the common good, as Michael Sandel has illustrated, is one of the key drivers behind the urge to control or regulate markets better, as well as the desire to deliver public benefits and services through non-market means. Scepticism about whether there is such a thing as the common good can lead some Liberals to be more biased in favour of free markets where individuals can make their own bargains.

All Liberals are passionate about free trade but differ over what they want to treat as trade. Christians, perhaps following the example of Christ in the Temple, are more prone to question the scope and place of market behaviour and to encourage the state to do likewise.

Conclusion

Robust and rounded on human rights, engaged and empathetic on poverty, sceptical but supportive of state action; Christians have much to offer Liberalism.

There is however a perfectly coherent version of Liberalism that views society as a set of transactions between individuals pursuing their own good, made orderly but not influenced by the state; softened only by some redistribution of opportunity.

> **Robust and rounded on human rights, engaged and empathetic on poverty, sceptical but supportive of state action; Christians have much to offer Liberalism**

There are small Liberal parties on the continent that look like this. They are predominantly secular and not somewhere religious people feel at home.

However, the richness and indeed the strength of the British Liberal tradition has been its diversity – all attempts to narrow its ideological base have been politically disastrous.

Arguably too, the lack of confidence of its Christian voice that once flowed effortlessly from pulpit to parliament has actually weakened the party's appeal. That voice with its emphasis on human dignity, the fight against poverty and the public good seems as relevant now as it did in the days of Lloyd George or Gladstone. It is time to speak now or forever hold one's peace.

Notes:

1 *The Telegraph, 04 May 2003 http://www.telegraph.co.uk/news/uknews/1429109/Campbell-interrupted-Blair-as-he-spoke-of-his-faith-We-dont-do-God.html*

2 *Paul Marshall and David Laws (eds), The Orange Book: Reclaiming Liberalism (Profile Books, 2004)*

3 *Michael Sandel, What money can't buy: the moral limits of markets (Farrar, Straus and Giroux, 2012)*

2
What is Christianity, do I need to take it seriously, and can I be a Liberal Democrat and a Christian?

Tim Farron MP
MP for Westmorland and Lonsdale

People think that if you call yourself a Christian you are saying that you are a 'good person'; that it's a kind of moral form of showing off. Either that or it means that you believe in following all sorts of arcane rules, or that you are a needy person who can't cope with the world as it is and thus have to put your faith in a convenient deity. Declaring yourself a Christian, when you are in Liberal circles, also puts you in danger of being deemed a right wing moral authoritarian. At best, being a Christian is seen to mean believing in niceness and a kind of fuzzy, gentle philosophy which is equally harmless and useless.

It may of course be convenient to draw these conclusions, but they aren't true.

To be a Christian is to accept that Jesus Christ existed, that he made the amazing claim to be God and the only route to eternal life, and that those claims were true. If this last sentence is accurate, then, to be blunt, our personal opinions of Christians and Christianity are completely irrelevant because Jesus Christ's life, death and resurrection would then become the most significant events in the history of the universe – and how you respond to these facts would be the most important decision you will ever need to make.

So, what do Christians believe?
Well, that God created a perfect world, that human beings have selfishly turned away from God and tainted that perfect creation, that God is a

completely fair and just God and will justly judge all of us for our sin. Now, let's explain what sin is: it's rejecting God's good and loving rule and choosing to put ourselves in his place. The kind of things we do to reject God's rule over our lives differs from person to person, but the desire to push God out of our lives is the same in everyone. On that basis, we are all sinners and so none of us can look forward to God's just and fair judgement with any sense that we'll be OK. Luckily for us, God isn't only just and fair, he is also good, kind and merciful. He planned a way of sparing us by sending his only Son, Jesus, who took all of our sins on himself and died in our place – something that was God's intention since before creation.

He was the perfect and ultimate sacrifice. This means that anyone who puts their trust in this Jesus, will stand before God 'clothed' in Jesus' goodness and purity, just as Jesus clothed himself in our rottenness and sin. This is the ultimate act of real love – Jesus was punished for our sin, and he did it willingly, not grudgingly. He did it because he loves us. Now, all we need to do to know that we can face judgement with confidence is to accept that we are a 'sinner', say sorry to God and ask for his forgiveness, and accept Jesus as the perfect payment for every wrong thing we ever did.

So being a Christian is not about being good, indeed it's about facing up to the fact that we are the opposite of good. It's not about following arcane rules, because we are saved by God's mercy and not by a laborious process of ticking boxes and passing a kind of moral test. Perhaps it is about being needy – because each of us is needy. To re-use a cliché, everyone has a 'God-shaped hole inside them' which we try to fill with career, hedonism, relationships, addictions, money, material things in general, and other things that we turn into our own home-made little gods. We are all needy, and we meet our needs too often with counterfeit gods who do not satisfy. To be a Christian is to submit to ultimate truth, fairness and goodness – some of which will jar a little with our current state of socialisation. To be a Christian is to seek to be a radical, to be anti-establishment, anti-materialistic, anti-greed, other-centred not self-centred, humble not proud, self-controlled not controlled by selfish desires... and if you are a Christian you will also know that you will fail on a daily basis to live up to all of this. But to be a Christian is to humbly kneel before God and confess those failures in the certain knowledge that God will forgive you, because he promised to. Unlike politicians, God always keeps his promises.

So how did I come to accept all this?

I am a liberal, sceptical, fairly worldly kind of person. I grew up in a Guardian-reading, liberal-minded home. I was brought up to ask questions and not accept everything that was presented to me as truth as necessarily being so. I am, I guess, not the kind of person who easily falls for religion. And yet I became a Christian.

> **I became a Christian because the evidence for Christianity is staggeringly compelling**

I became a Christian because the evidence for Christianity is staggeringly compelling. Of course, becoming a Christian is staggeringly inconvenient too, which I suspect is why I buried my head in the sand for so long. If I was to become a Christian, I would have to accept that I was not the master of my own destiny; that I needed to bow down to the God who created me and who will judge me. I would also have to accept that I was a 'sinner' and ask for forgiveness and turn to Him as my master.

Is the evidence really all that compelling? Yes, I'd say so. Let's see if I can deal with the evidence for Christ in a few quick paragraphs (it really needs a few volumes!). First, there's prophecy. Most of us know that the New Testament is all about Jesus Christ, but if you look carefully you will see that the same can also be said about the Old Testament. There are around 320 individual predictions relating to the coming of the Messiah (Messiah is Hebrew for 'Christ', and Christ is Greek for 'God's chosen King'). They relate, for example, to where the Messiah would be born (Bethlehem), which family line he would come through (David), how he would die (crucifixion), his social standing (relative poverty), the timing of his life and death (during the relatively brief time that the second temple was standing in Jerusalem), and the way in which he would be received by the leaders of his day. You can check for yourself, but all 320 predictions come true in Jesus and no one else. The odds against this happening by accident are extremely slim! Of course some people will choose to believe that this is all just coincidence. All I can say is, "I wish I had your faith..!"

Second, let's look at the reliability of the written evidence. The evidence is pretty clear now that all of the New Testament was written by 100 AD. Some of it was written by the late 40s AD. There are many references to eye witness accounts within the Gospels – for example, when Jesus healed Jairus' daughter, or raised Lazarus from the dead after four days, friends and family are described as being present at these events – and they would still have been alive at the point that these accounts were circulated. Many of the stories relate to specific people in specific places, and so if the accounts had not been true, there were hundreds of people around to contradict them – but they did not do so.

If someone were to write an account of the 1987 General Election and claim that David Owen had come out in favour of unilateral nuclear disarmament (he wasn't by the way, quite the opposite!), the eye witnesses still with us would have contradicted this and killed off the account. Remember too that 'history is written by the winners' – only the early Christians were definitely not the winners! The Christians in 33AD were a tiny, persecuted group who were up against the power and might of the religious establishment and the Roman Empire. Both of these organisations had vast motivation to disprove Christianity, to produce an un-resurrected body of Jesus, to produce evidence that the resurrection didn't happen, to develop a counter narrative to kill off the Christian church. This should have been a very easy job. They had all the resources they needed to kill off a lie, a rumour or a legend. But for some reason they failed and today the death of a carpenter in an obscure corner of the Roman Empire 2,000 years ago remains the most celebrated and talked about event in human history.

Remember too that there are in existence something like 20,000 manuscript copies of the New Testament documents – the earliest of which dates to around 60 years after the death of the last eye witnesses.[1] Compare this with the fact that there are just 10 existing copies of Caesar's account of the Gallic Wars, the earliest of which dates to 1,000 years after the death of the last eye witness. No one seriously challenges the authenticity of Caesar's work, and yet many dismiss Christianity as a myth or a lie – why? Well, if you will forgive me for being mildly cynical, it's because it would be very inconvenient if Christianity turned out to be true. If Caesar's account of the Gallic Wars is true, it doesn't mean that you have to change your life one jot. If Christ is real, it changes everything.

Third, let's look at the circumstantial evidence surrounding the behaviour of Jesus' followers. After Judas' betrayal, the eleven remaining disciples pretty much went into hiding – we read of Peter disowning Jesus and of Thomas refusing to believe that Jesus had risen from the dead. We know that they were on the whole a pretty flaky bunch (I'd have been much worse I'm sure). Yet just a few weeks later, this rather pathetic group who had seen their leader killed and their hopes smashed, was transformed into a fearless team of individuals who boldly proclaimed that Jesus was the Christ, that he had risen from the dead and that he was the Saviour of the world.

Why the transformation? With the exception of John, who died an old man in Roman captivity, all of the disciples demonstrated staggering bravery, getting themselves executed or murdered for proclaiming that the resurrection had happened and that Jesus was who he said he was. What are the chances of this happening if Jesus wasn't the Christ? Think of it this way: when the 9/11 bombers murdered more than 3,000 innocent people in America, they did so believing that they were committing a holy act of martyrdom and that they would wake up in Paradise. They received their beliefs second hand, so if they died for a lie (and I am convinced that they did) then they did not know it was a lie. However, if Jesus' disciples died for a lie, then they were eye witnesses and they would have known it was a lie. How likely is it that they would have done that?

People are of course completely entitled to draw their own conclusions from all this, but I would simply suggest that the evidence for Jesus Christ is at the very least credible; that Christianity is therefore intellectually plausible and, given that the consequences of Christianity being true are pretty massive, you owe it to yourself to check it out for yourself.

Why Christians should engage with politics

For many Christians, politics is a dirty business and they prefer to stay out of it. I would argue that Christians should be involved in politics – Peter's first letter calls on Christians to engage with politics. Personally I spend much more of my life doing things for the Liberal Democrats than I do for church. To quote Ecclesiastes, "whatever your hand finds to do, do it with all your might", which is a call to accept whatever calling or job you have and completely put your back into it as an act of service to God and to others.[2]

> **To quote Ecclesiastes, "whatever your hand finds to do, do it with all your might", which is a call to accept whatever calling or job you have and completely put your back into it as an act of service to God and to others**

Furthermore, as Christians we are called to be different from the world but we are also called to involve ourselves in it and to act with kindness, honesty and gentleness. When I read the book of Amos in the Old Testament I am reminded that while Christians are called to be meek on their own behalf, they are called to be strident when it comes to the injustices suffered by others. That is one of the many reasons why I see being a Liberal Democrat and a Christian as entirely consistent.

Because Christians have a sure hope in a sinless, deathless, perfect new creation where peace reigns, we are motivated in this life to live lives of justice, peace and service to others now. This is why so much of our voluntary sector stems from the church, why it should surprise no one that the movement to abolish slavery was led by committed Christians and why the movements against industrial squalor and the mistreatment of children in the 19th Century were led almost exclusively by Christians. It is these very movements that gave the Liberal Party its purpose from our earliest days.

Of course, all the main political parties in Britain are secular – and rightly so – which means that our policies will not generally or automatically reflect Christian themes. But our policies do focus on protecting the poor and the vulnerable, standing up against exploitation of the powerless by the powerful, seeking truth beyond serving powerful vested interests, providing careful stewardship for our environment, serving those who are in need as opposed to the comfortable, and protecting the rights of minorities (and Christians need to remember that they belong to a minority!). In seeking to direct our economy in a way which is balanced and not yielding to ideology, I would say that we are seeking to demonstrate not only justice and fairness but also wisdom.

The Bible says many things that society will feel uncomfortable about with regards to personal morality. Given that Christians accept the Bible as the word of the perfect God and that we are

> **We must never seek to legislate to force people who are not Christians to live as if they were**

extremely imperfect human beings, then we should be surprised if the Bible doesn't make us uncomfortable! But I also believe that we must never seek to legislate to force people who are not Christians to live as if they were.

Going back to the birth of the Liberal Party, our history is one of defending the rights of the non-conformist Christians – we'd call them 'low church' or evangelicals today. But our history is also based on championing the rights of all oppressed and under-represented groups. We may not all agree with one another but we stand or fall together and we surely believe in the right to individual conscience and the right for individuals to speak their mind freely, without fear of restriction or penalty. The evidence is that the other parties in Britain have regularly sought to restrict freedom – whether it be through 90 days' detention without trial, restrictions on the right to move to a different country, or threats to our right to privacy in electronic communications. Liberal Democrats stand alone as the defender of the rights of all human beings, especially those we might refer to as 'outsider' and oppressed groups.

Conclusion

As Christians we should be motivated to live out our faith in practice, and that includes acting to meet the needs of others, to stand up for those who have least, to promote justice, to argue against complacency in the face of injustice, to seek wisdom when it comes to being in authority, to ensure that decisions are taken wisely and fairly – not in order to satisfy powerful vested interests – and to ensure that government and politics are conducted with kindness, goodness and gentleness.

Christians are never encouraged to remove themselves from society, to sit in seclusion and either ignore it or condemn it. Instead we are called to get our hands dirty, while keeping our hearts pure

Christians are never encouraged to remove themselves from society, to sit in seclusion and either ignore it or condemn it. Instead we are called to get our hands dirty, while keeping our hearts pure. Fairer taxes; a greener Britain; action to deal with an economic recovery caused by unrestricted greed; an economic plan built on wisdom rather than dogma; action to protect and defend asylum seekers, those who find themselves out of work, and others who are struggling to get by; action to stop wealthy and powerful media barons getting away with persecuting the innocent; action to increase the state pension by its largest ever amount. These are things I do motivated by being both a Liberal Democrat and a Christian.

It is perfectly possible to belong to pretty much any mainstream political party and be a Christian. Likewise, being involved in any political party ought to give Christians reasons to feel uncomfortable at times. But I would argue that it is entirely consistent for me to be a committed Christian and a lifelong dedicated Liberal Democrat too. I'd encourage you to join me on both counts!

Notes:

1 F.F. Bruce, *The New Testament Documents: Are They Reliable?* (InterVarsity Press, 1981)

2 *Ecclesiastes 9:10, New International Version*

3
Liberalism, the Liberal Democrats and the dangerous drift towards moral conformity

Greg Mulholland MP
MP for Leeds North West

During the last general election campaign in 2010, I was out knocking on doors in the terraced red brick streets of Headingley and Hyde Park, in the south of my constituency. Things were going very well, the response was generally very positive, and the excitement of Cleggmania palpable amongst many of the students who lived in this part of Leeds. Many houses were agreeing to put up a poster; others were enthusiastically giving me and the Liberal Democrats their support. When I was knocking at one house, however, a group of a few students, male and female, came out from a house I had called at a few minutes before, and started chanting at me. A rhyme about my being a Catholic and about where I could shove my rosary beads. I have never been on the receiving end of discriminatory hatred before and it is, even for a thick skinned politician, a really unpleasant experience.

The outburst had been stirred up by the most unlikely of sources – my Conservative opponent – who had distributed a leaflet painting me as something like a right wing, intolerant and authoritarian Christian zealot in a desperate attempt to gain some votes. It was unsuccessful, and the Conservative result was the worst ever since the creation of the seat. But it was an experience I will never forget. As a Christian, if I am to follow Christ's teaching, I must be grateful to those who abuse me in his name. Indeed, whilst wrong and at the time surprisingly unpleasant, it has given me a much better understanding of what it is like to face hatred as a result of what you are, and an appreciation of the experiences of others who face racial, sexist, homophobic or nationalistic hatred.

As a Liberal, however, I am disgusted by hatred of all kinds and here I was the victim of some pretty unpleasant religious hatred. The hypocrisy of this behaviour was that this group of people would similarly disagree with many Muslims and many Jews on certain 'moral' issues as we call them. Yet would they troop out into the street to abuse a Jewish or Muslim candidate? Especially if they were not white? For some educated and politically involved people, anti-Christian hatred, and in particular it seems, anti-Catholic bigotry, 187 years after Catholic emancipation, is somehow quite acceptable.

All three main political parties have always had Christians as members, supporters and representatives. Yet the clear message for this nasty sub-campaign, having read the leaflets that were distributed, was that I was not allowed, publicly at least, to let my faith influence my politics, indeed that I was not allowed to be a Christian MP.

Liberalism, the Liberal Democrats and religious tolerance

What this taught me was not only that anti-Christian hatred remains alive and well in our country but worse than that, it showed that there are some who claim to be progressive but who think that this particular form of prejudice, of hatred and of bigotry is perfectly acceptable. Now, no doubt this house full of students (both sexes, all white, all it seemed middle class) were probably Labour supporters. Yet their naked hatred and football hooligan style abuse was reserved for my faith, not my politics. They would not have told me where I could shove my copy of J.S. Mill's On Liberty. As a group of educated people, they could presumably somehow justify their behaviour, because of my faith and because of them presumably not supporting my party either.

The question that I asked myself though was another more pertinent one, to me. Would any similarly educated people who called themselves liberals, indeed possibly even Liberal Democrats, ever behave in the same way?

Of course, I would hope not. Indeed I am confident that no Liberal Democrat supporter, never mind member, would ever deem such clearly nasty behaviour as acceptable. Yet the attitude that lies behind it seems alas all too common in our party. That many long held Christian views are no longer allowed within the party and that on some issues, there is only one view, to be accepted, without challenge or criticism.

There is a dangerous and almost imperceptible drift that has taken place in the Liberal Democrats in recent years, a drift away from tolerance, of acceptance of religions and faiths, alongside secular belief systems like humanism, towards a moral conformity. A moral conformity that certain views are part of who we are; and that many faith based, Christian views are rather something to be reserved for private worship that should be kept firmly out of the political arena. It may not be as obviously discriminatory as the abuse I experienced during that election campaign, but it is nevertheless equally damaging and illiberal. The received wisdom amongst too many Liberal Democrats, from MPs and peers to the wider membership, seems to be this: believe what we believe when it comes to 'moral' issues or issues of conscience, or you are not a Liberal Democrat. The trouble with that view is that it is not only illiberal. It is the very antithesis of liberalism.

> **There is a dangerous and almost imperceptible drift that has taken place in the Liberal Democrats in recent years, a drift away from tolerance, of acceptance of religions and faiths, alongside secular belief systems like humanism, towards a moral conformity**

Let me be clear: as a liberal I believe everyone has the right to think that what I believe faith-wise is bunkum and nonsense. They have every right to say so publicly if they wish without fear of criminal prosecution for blasphemy or religious hatred (I am assuming any liberal would make their views on my faith in a temperate and respectful way even if they fundamentally disagree with my beliefs!). But nevertheless, as long as without threat, abuse or hatred, they are entitled to do so! Indeed I would fight for their right to do so. But I fear that what we are heading towards now in the party is away from freedom of conscience and towards a new moral conformity, and it is a dangerous trend.

This drift became apparent during the debate over the Marriage (Same Sex Couples) Bill. While a policy in favour of the principle of marriage for same-sex couples had been passed at party conference some time before, it was rightly agreed that there should be a 'free vote' for Parliamentarians on this issue, since it was considered to be a matter of conscience. And yet many in the party clearly did not treat it as such. Freedom of conscience seemed to be pushed out of the debate, and anyone who dared to do or say anything but wave a simplistic 'pro equal marriage' banner was deemed to be intolerant, 'against' gay rights, and actually therefore against the party and 'liberalism'. I had tweets and emails from some in the party telling me that I MUST support this at all costs, without scrutiny or question; and certainly that I must ignore any views that might stem from my faith. I heard MP colleagues who decided according to their own consciences that they should vote against the bill being pilloried by fellow MPs. One Liberal Democrat Minister referred to 'the God squad' in a derisory fashion.

The ironic thing was that my personal reasons for abstaining in the second reading, and supporting some of the amendments at third reading, was in fact because I felt the bill was badly drafted and not liberal enough. Indeed a liberal perspective would have taken this debate back further, to look at the confused history of legal marriage, its religious basis and whether this is the right starting point for reform or whether a more fundamental, more radical change was sensible. I was in favour of equal legal recognition for all, but objected to the fact that the bill provided two different definitions of civil marriage not one; it continues to deny the same pension rights to same-sex civil partners; and prevents humanists and some religions having civil marriage ceremonies. I instead argued for separation of civil and religious marriage and complete freedom of conscience for all as well as exact equal legal rights, legal definition and legal status for all. Sadly the debate

> **It was rightly agreed that there should be a 'free vote' for Parliamentarians on this issue, since it was considered to be a matter of conscience. And yet many in the party clearly did not treat it as such**

turned from being about 'how does the state best equally recognise all adult consensual relationships?' to 'are you an enthusiastic champion of gay marriage or are you intolerant and bigoted?' Many in the party seemed to confuse the admirable fight for gay rights with the adoption of a position that everyone has to share the same idea of marriage or the same way to achieve legal recognition for all adult couples. The fact that the Government's bill was a deeply confused and flawed one, that neither delivers equality nor adequately protects freedom of conscience, did not seem to matter. You are either with us or against us.

That is not liberal and not the way liberals do things.

"Don't try to impose your religious views on me!!"

I had a conversation with a fellow Liberal Democrat MP in the Members' dining room in the House of Commons, around the time of the second reading of the Marriage Bill, when he told fellow diners with some glee how, in reply to an email he had received from a local bishop, he had firmly responded, "please don't try to impose your views on me".

Alas this seems to be a very common reaction by many in our party when faced with lobbying on an issue that has a link to faith-based (and specifically Christian) teachings. Yet the same people say nothing about those who seek to impose their views on, say, the killing of badgers, or how far disabled people have to walk to get certain benefits, or whether or not we should leave the EU. MPs are constantly being lobbied by all sorts of people – constituents, organisations, party members and the wider public – all seeking to influence the MP's thinking and decision-making on a variety of topics. This is quite right, and a vital aspect of democracy. They often speak their mind forcefully and with great passion. But MPs do not respond to all lobbyists with the phrase "please don't try to impose your views on me". To suggest that people are only imposing their view when the matter in question is a 'moral issue' is simply not true. Either none of them are, or they all are. Furthermore, if those against same-sex marriage were seeking to 'impose' their view on their MP, then those who spoke equally passionately in favour of it were also doing exactly the same. To fail to recognise that – and to only suggest that religious people do or even are capable of doing so – sadly exposes an inherent illiberal prejudice against religion and those who choose to follow one. Both sides had every right to lobby their MP, yet for some, one set of emails was acceptable (because they agreed with them) and another set was not.

The attitude displayed by this and by comments made all too often along these lines, also shows a fundamental lack of understanding or respect of religions, as belief systems (which is of course a lack of understanding or respect of religion itself). We are told, "Of course you have the right to believe whatever you want; just don't allow it to influence your views!"

The fact is that all of us in politics who believe in something (and that should be all of us!) are of course seeking to follow those beliefs to do our bit for our fellow citizens and society. This idea that seeking to influence opinions and outcomes is wrong (but only when there is any possibility 'God' may be involved) forgets the whole purpose of politics. Would anyone take anyone seriously if they said to us, "I respect your views as a liberal, just please don't try to impose your liberal views on others".

Would anyone take anyone seriously if they said to us, "I respect your views as a liberal, just please don't try to impose your liberal views on others"

That would be patently ridiculous. Liberals – and socialist and conservatives and all other political groupings – exist precisely to seek to get elected, then to impose their view of society upon it and all living in it! When the party leaders stand up at election time, they are saying very clearly, "This is my vision for our country and our society and I want enough of you to vote for me so that I and we can impose our philosophy, through related policies, on the rest because we think that is the best thing for the country and its people". It's called representative majority based democracy, which is the most popular system of government in the world, but the system is based on the very premise that the majority (and in truth not actually a majority of voters) can impose their will on the whole population.

For some in our party, their 'Liberal Democracy' seems less and less a political philosophy, but more and more a rigid value system, a moral framework and increasingly (whether they realise it or not – and ironically) a pretty rigid one. Despite the historical roots of the party, there are too many in it who now think that Christians can't be Liberal Democrats, or not without ignoring their beliefs. They say, of course, that we can all believe what we wish, in private, but deny the right to pursue what we believe in, which is not only illiberal but is actually anti-religious – as doing so is what religion (and freedom to follow it) means! They seem to forget what our constitution says – that we "seek to balance the fundamental values of liberty, equality and community", not to pursue or prioritise one at the expense of others, and certainly not to demand 'equality' or 'sameness' at all costs; that is the preserve of the intolerant left. It seems alas that a growing number of Liberal Democrats also believe that, and have therefore lost that balance.

Religious tolerance (genuine religious tolerance as opposed to tokenistic religious tolerance) means by its very nature, accepting that certain people, through their faith, have a view of how people should live their lives and how society should best be run, for the benefit of all. Religion is not and never has been a private thing. So denying people the right to act, to speak and to vote according to conscience is actually a denial of religious freedom and is intolerance of what religion actually is. Intolerant secularism is utterly inconsistent with liberalism, yet there is a creeping sense in the party that this is the only natural synergy. If that trend continues, the Liberal Democrats could no longer be seen as a place where people of faith feel comfortable; and if these people are pushed out, it will be a tragedy not just for all Christian liberals who would no longer have a home, but also damaging to a party that wants – and needs – to have a broad appeal electorally.

Being a Christian involved in politics doesn't mean telling people to believe in God. It means showing them that Christianity, if followed and put into practice, is a positive force for good. I don't tell people they have to be a liberal (which would not be liberal!) but I do indeed tell them about the liberal values I believe in, about the ways to pursue them and about how doing so will be in the interest of our country, our society and our communities. In the same way, Christians who are liberals must not push their faith onto others, but rather tell people about the positive, compassionate, justice-seeking, Christ-given vision of the world, which if delivered in the way he intended, will help our country, our society, our communities and the whole family of humankind.

What does Liberal Democrat philosophy say?

If I dare make the analogy, a little like a Christian looking at the Gospels, or a Muslim at the Koran, let us look at our inspiration, our philosophical underpinning. Consider what that wonderful and often quoted Preamble to the Liberal Democrat Constitution, of which we are – from all backgrounds, cultures and belief systems – so rightly proud, says about matters of faith.

"We champion the freedom, dignity and well-being of individuals; we acknowledge and respect their right to freedom of conscience"

"We look forward to a world...in which their different cultures will be able to develop freely"

"We reject all prejudice and discrimination based upon race, colour, religion, age, disability, sex or sexual orientation"

"We will at all times defend the right to speak, write, worship, associate and vote freely"

We want to build a society "in which no one shall be enslaved by poverty, ignorance or conformity"

These are statements of which we should be proud. We profess to believe in freedom of conscience, and we must uphold it. We wish to see different cultures developing freely – which means not just Diaspora communities but the various cultures within our own society, including the different branches of Christianity – whether Methodist, Presbyterian, Catholic or others. We stand against prejudice – and we must remember that it is wrong not just when it is against Islam, Hinduism, or other world religions; it is also wrong when directed against Christianity. We defend the right to worship – and this must include allowing people the right to express their faith through the whole of their lives. To defend only the right to 'worship', but not the right to 'believe' and to 'express' that belief, would be a sham. Religion has never meant just spending an hour in a building once a week (even if for some it does mean that!). It means believing something, attempting (and sometimes failing) to adhere to those beliefs and expressing those views when it is believed important to do so – notably when challenged or faced with a situation where those beliefs are tested or required to help judge a particular situation. Finally, we are non-conformists – we acknowledge that no-one should be enslaved by conforming to others.

Well here's the nub. There is a worrying trend in the liberal party of British politics, that whilst we rightly all rail against poverty and ignorance, and in theory against conformity, there are too many in our party who seek to impose a new conformity on others. The new secularist conformity is exactly what people, including some within our own party, and increasingly in society, are seeking to impose on others and by so doing to enslave them.

A proud liberal and a good Christian?

I am certainly a proud liberal and I try to be a good Christian (and even though I all too often fail to achieve the latter, I do insist on my right to be allowed to be a Christian). The real question at the heart of this debate is whether we can be a good Christian, and proud of our faith, and proud to be a Liberal Democrat. The answer to that at the moment for many is unclear.

I am a liberal not in spite of my faith. I am a liberal not just alongside my faith. I am a liberal because of my faith. So anyone who denies me my right to believe in Jesus Christ is denying me of my right to believe in liberalism. That philosophical path is the road to intolerance, to undermining freedom of conscience, a road that no true liberal would proceed along.

> **I am a liberal not in spite of my faith. I am a liberal not just alongside my faith. I am a liberal because of my faith**

Liberals are often accused of moral relativism, especially by the political right, who like to portray liberalism as saying 'anything goes'. In fact, nothing could be further from the truth. It is precisely because real liberalism is a strong belief system, with a clear and powerful view of how people should treat others and how society is best ordered, that many of us, whether we believe in God, a god, gods or no gods, are proud to call ourselves, and to be, liberals. That liberalism is something that fits just as well with a positive Christian view of society and humanity as with a positive humanist view. Liberalism must remain at the heart of the Liberal Democrats and therefore continue to be the reason why Christians, as well as those of other faiths and none, decide to join, to campaign, and to stand.

I would never ever join or support a party that aligned itself to a certain faith. I would never be a Christian Democrat, whether such a party were liberal or not; but equally Christians who are liberals cannot feel comfortable in any party that tells them that their Christianity has no role in public life and denies them their very reason for wanting to help their society and their community.

Conclusion – the future for personal belief, Liberalism and the Liberal Democrats

So it is time to halt this dangerous and fundamentally illiberal drift to moral conformity that is creeping into the party. We need strong leadership at all levels in the party, from the leader down, to ensure that the Liberal Democrats remains a party that welcomes people of all world religions. There are millions of people who have a faith in Britain – whether Christian, Jewish, Muslim or another – and to neglect to engage with them would be to become a factional party and not the mainstream party that it professes to be, that listens to and engages with people of all backgrounds.

I have hope that our party will address this, and restore freedom of conscience to its rightful place at the heart of the party. Liberals come in all shapes, sizes, genders, nationalities, races, sexual preferences; from all backgrounds; and from all major belief systems. We include Christians, of all kinds, Anglicans, Catholics, Methodists, Baptists, Unitarians, Pentecostals, Quakers, Jews, Muslims, Hindus, Bahá'ís, Sikhs, humanists, agnostics, atheists, secularists and more. But we are all liberals; and long, I hope and pray, may we all remain Liberal Democrats.

4
Three Reasons to Thank God
– and not the usual ones

Sir Andrew Stunell MP
MP for Hazel Grove

Let's start by thanking God that we live in a secular and pluralist society
Not one where the rule of law is set by the whim of an ayatollah, or the rage of a Cromwell. Not one where we take turns to burn each other at the stake. But a society where, with freedom of conscience and action, we can each worship God as we see fit, practise our faith openly, and take a full part in the lively determination of our country's future without let or hindrance regardless of our beliefs.

It wasn't always like that, despite the myth that there was once a golden age of Christian faith and tolerance in our country that the coming of atheists and Muslims has undermined. Go back to William Wilberforce's classic battle to end the slave trade. Isn't that the perfect example of Christian moral leadership setting our nation on the path of righteousness?

In reality the story of Wilberforce raises two powerful challenges for 21st Century Christians who hanker for those good old days. First, has it ever occurred to you to ask why not one of the Methodist and Catholic MPs stood alongside Wilberforce in that battle to end the slave trade?

Think a bit harder. That's right; there weren't any Methodist or Catholic MPs. Only members of the Church of England could enter the House back then. Indeed, my Baptist forefathers had to flee to Holland in 1611 to escape Anglican persecution, and there published the first ever English-language plea for universal religious tolerance; Thomas Helwys' 'Mystery of Iniquity' asserting the right of every man to worship God in his own way – "even Turks, Catholics and Jews".[1] On his return to England, King James I imprisoned Helwys for life for his treasonous opinions. It took another 215 years before (Anglican) MPs would vote to let others join them in the House.

So we never have been all one great big happy Christian family. That's the first reality to confront about the Wilberforce years and our spurious claims of unique English tolerance. Liberals cannot afford to be smug either. Read Gladstone on Roman Catholicism, and blush!

But that is not the biggest challenge of the Wilberforce story for Christians by a long way. The biggest challenge is for us to explain why Wilberforce was right about slavery, and St Paul was wrong. Take another look at the Epistle to Philemon. Imagine that a young man turned up on your church steps one day to say that he'd run away from the neighbouring fruit-picking farm where he'd been held captive without pay for years. Would you (a) notify the police or (b) give him a letter to take back to the farmer asking for him not to be treated too harshly for running away? I'm guessing, but I think you are on Wilberforce's side on this one. But why not St Paul's? That's where I want to give more thanks to God.

Let's thank God that the Holy Spirit has been at work through the ages

Some of us think that it wasn't only slavery where St Paul hadn't fully discerned the Spirit. But whether the priesthood of all believers includes women or not can perhaps wait for another day. My point is that the Holy Spirit didn't stop work when the Book of Revelation was sealed. Not according to Scripture itself, and not according to the subsequent evidence – of which Wilberforce's successful crusade is a landmark piece, and Thomas Helwys' plea is another.

So no Christian should have as their goal the recreation of some mythical olden-days society where Christian values were understood and universally acknowledged, where lambs and lions sat down together, and harmony reigned supreme. It never has existed. Neither the first century in Judea nor the 19th Century in England provides that model.

Of course no Christian I've ever met would truly want to live in one of those earlier societies. For the very good reason that, thanks to the vigorous and continuing work of God's Holy Spirit, we know better than they did. Not just about slavery, but about children's rights, care of the disabled, respect for differences, being a lot more relaxed about women wearing hats and veils in church... The list is a very long one, and it is interesting that some Christians now use these very new revelations of God's will as the touchstones to judge other religions by. A lack of respect for women's rights, imposed modesty of dress, and savage intolerance of dissident beliefs are characteristics now being pinned on Islam to discredit it. By Christians! All the things we took 500 or more years of bloody history to put behind us they somehow expect to be absorbed everywhere else in a blink of an eye. But that isn't my main point. My main point is that the Holy Spirit hasn't stopped yet. So to my third thanksgiving:

Let's thank God that he has yet more truth to break forth from his Word

For the Holy Spirit is still at work, post Wilberforce, post votes for women, showing us how God wants our society, nationally and internationally to be shaped. It's contentious, it's rough edged, it's uneven, but it is happening. Certainly, it's not going to be put right everywhere in the blink of an eye. But there is a world-wide movement towards the recognition that if all six billion of us are made in God's image, we must all be treated equally and honestly by each other, our huge differences of belief and culture and of everything else notwithstanding.

There is a world-wide movement towards the recognition that if all six billion of us are made in God's image, we must all be treated equally and honestly by each other, our huge differences of belief and culture and of everything else notwithstanding

That has found its international expression most formally in the

United Nations Declaration of Human Rights. Not only have most of the nations with a Christian cultural background endorsed it, so have most of the others. What both it, and they, are acknowledging is the worth of humankind, and the task entrusted to each of us to treat the other with respect and fairness (if not exactly love) both individually and at the collective and national levels. Of course there's a long way to go from 'declaration' to 'implementation', especially in some countries and some cultures. It might easily take another 215 years. But what it and its derivatives, like our own Human Rights Act, assert is that there is no excuse or rational belief that allows us to think of one group of human beings as inferior to another, or can legitimise their persecution or justify deliberate discrimination against them.

This means full rights for women worldwide. Family rights, educational rights, employment rights, property rights, democratic rights. Every right that a man should have. Hardly controversial to this readership, I would suppose. And please note the important point that giving women their rights doesn't make people more likely to be women.

It means full rights for disabled people. Family rights, educational rights, employment rights, property rights, democratic rights. Just note, too, that the existence of those rights for disabled people doesn't make more people disabled – though it does make them more visible, and properly acknowledged and better provided for than they were in this country even twenty years ago.

It means full rights for gay people. Family rights, educational rights, employment rights, property rights, democratic rights. And again, please note that allowing gay people their rights doesn't make more people gay. Though of course they will be more visible and properly acknowledged.

You knew there was going to be a catch, I'm sure. Women and disabled people, fair enough, but gay people is going too far, say some. There were Christian opponents of Wilberforce who feared the end of the slave trade would bring the collapse of their Jamaican sugar estates, undermine the Diocesan finances and reduce funding for evangelism. They appealed endlessly to Scripture to justify themselves, even pointing out that the slaves had the gospel preached to them in Jamaica which they never would have had if they'd been left in African barbarity. Apart from that, they weren't fully human. Today we writhe and squirm at such sophistry. Or do we? There were staunch Christians who opposed votes for women, too – and for that matter in generations before, opposed every social reform and advance for the last 2,000 years. In this generation it is rights for gay people that seem so hard to acknowledge and so readily denied.

> **In this generation it is rights for gay people that seem so hard to acknowledge and so readily denied**

In contrast to that, in all my years as an MP and a councillor I have never once had a letter from any Christian asking me to make committing adultery a criminal offence, or to introduce a law to stop adulterers adopting children, or prevent them teaching children, or repeal the Civil Marriage Act that permits them to remarry, or to require them to have medical treatment to prevent a recurrence of their sexual behaviour. I have had all of those things recommended to me about gay people. That is despite the fact that adultery is unambiguously condemned in Scripture in a way that goes far beyond the somewhat iffy references dredged up about gay behaviour. It unambiguously causes far more harm to far more children than gay behaviour, and is unambiguously very much more damaging and destabilising to families, and of course the institution of marriage, and society at large. Just ask any MP about their Child Support Agency caseload.

So why aren't Christian letter-writers on at their MPs about adultery all the time? For the same reason that pedestrians think the dangers on our roads are caused by speeding cars, motorists think the real sinners are reckless cyclists, and cyclists blame HGVs. Most of us are heterosexual, so we just don't see adultery as being as threatening to society as a gay relationship. Then again, when the census reports that half of all couples are unmarried, including perhaps our own children or grandchildren, it really all gets too close to home. So why not write a letter to the MP about gay marriage instead. To me that looks like displacement activity, or worse.

I rejoice that we live in a secular society where we can provide a secure and respectful place for everyone. So I'm not in favour of criminalising adultery or cohabitation, of going back to the Witches of Salem, or Calvin in Geneva or Cromwell and the Commonwealth. Nor of repealing our divorce laws, which objectively present a more terminal threat to marriage than do any gay rights. Nor of restricting law-making only to those who assent to the 39 Articles. Nor of sending slaves back to their masters. And when most Christians think carefully about it, nor are they in favour of these things either. Is that them giving in to feeble liberal relativism, or is it the Holy Spirit at work in them? It's time for each one of us to decide.

Making Christians angry is easy. Making Christians think is the hard part

Perhaps this will anger some people. Thomas Helwys made James I angry. Wilberforce made the Bishops angry. Making Christians angry is easy. Making Christians think is the hard part.

Notes:

1 Thomas Helwys, *A Short Declaration of the Mystery of Iniquity (1612)*

Part Two:
How should we 'do God'?

5
Should the State Forgive?

Sir Alan Beith MP
MP for Berwick-upon-Tweed

Forgiveness, following repentance, is at the centre of the Christian world view. Everyone who recites the Lord's Prayer reasserts the principle that if God forgives us, we should forgive those who do harm to us. But what if you are a magistrate, a judge, a police officer, a party policy-maker or a Government minister? Should you be putting Christian principles into practice by dispensing forgiveness to those who have harmed others, even if the victims or, more often, the public in general demand severe retribution? Is it a natural Liberal position to promote an approach which can be caricatured as 'soft' on crime, or is the espousal of forgiveness on behalf of society irresponsible as well as politically suicidal?

These are questions which go to the heart of the debate about sentencing policy, and I believe that Christian thinking has an important contribution to make to that debate. Heaven knows, we need such a debate – crime itself is reducing, but reoffending by those who go through our criminal justice system remains at ludicrously high levels.

What is sentencing meant to do? First of all, it is about the maintenance of public safety. No-one would challenge the view that serial murderers have to be locked away for most or even all of their lives in order to protect the public. Freedom from violent attack is as important a civil liberty as freedom from state oppression. Even if repentance and forgiveness can be envisaged in such cases, they do not take away the need for public protection and reassurance. But the majority of people in prison are not serial murderers or serial rapists. So why are so many people sent to prison, a higher proportion in Britain than in most other European countries?

In many people's minds, another significant purpose of sentencing, and particularly prison sentences, is as a deterrent to crime. However, as any acquaintance with the prison population will quickly convince you, deterrence is remarkably ineffective. Most people, when they commit crimes, do not believe they will be caught or, even if they are, that they will be found guilty or sent to prison. And many regular offenders do not see prison as the threat or the horror that it would seem to many of us – it is sometimes a tolerable refuge from a dysfunctional family and a disordered lifestyle. Offenders have told me that they committed further offences to escape a demanding community sentence – prison was an easier option.

So, if deterrence can be largely disproved, does that leave the way clear for a more 'Christian' approach to criminality, stressing the value of forgiveness? Not without examining another very significant aspect of sentencing. It is often unhelpfully referred to as retribution, a distinctly unchristian concept. What it really amounts to is the assertion by society of what is unacceptable and repugnant, and the 'ranking' of offences according to how seriously society views them. For example, anything less than a prison sentence seems not to be taking repeated violent offences seriously. If the punishment for a particularly brutal attack is less than for a lesser offence, they feel that society's values are not being expressed or enforced. This is an important issue and should not be dismissed by woolly pseudo-liberal thinking, even though its importance is undermined by selective and sensational tabloid reporting of particular sentences. "Attacker walks free" or, "Rapist will be free to strike again" are tempting headlines when the circumstances of the case can be ignored; although of course the courts do sometimes get it wrong.

But a bigger difficulty for rational sentencing policy is that prison, and the length of a prison sentence, is the only recognised measure in the public and media-influenced mind of how seriously an offence is being treated. That will remain a problem and a barrier to change until we can get people to understand, as many offenders already understand, that a demanding community sentence may be a far more significant punishment than a spell in prison with three meals a day and not a lot to do. I always remember a particularly successful reforming prison governor in Norway saying, "Prisons are full of people who have never faced up to their responsibility for the consequences of their actions: when we put them in prison, instead of forcing them to take on responsibility, we make sure that they are not responsible for anything at all". That brings us right back to Christian thinking. The Christian concept of forgiveness involves repentance – recognising and renouncing the wrong you have done. The criminal justice system should make people face up to the harmful consequences of their actions.

That is one of the great benefits of restorative justice, an approach which is firmly rooted in New Testament thinking. Restorative justice processes work to bring offenders and victims into communication, allowing victims

> **There are an increasing number of stories of forgiveness following restorative justice encounters**

to express the impact an offence has had upon them, as well as getting answers to their unanswered questions about the crime. It also gives the offender the opportunity to make amends. If the victim of a crime is able and willing to engage in the process, it can be a means by which offenders are forced to open their eyes to the reality of what they have done and the harm they have caused. It cannot be used in all cases, and no victim can ever be required to engage in it. The thought of it, and the anticipated pain of re-living the offence, is enough to put many people off, but it is surprising how many victims are willing to take the step. Almost all find it beneficial and there are an increasing number of stories of forgiveness following restorative justice encounters. It is a growing element in our criminal justice system, and an especially welcome one to Christians.

But before Christian idealists get too carried away, there are some things to remember about forgiveness. One is that we do not have the right to offer forgiveness for wrongs done to others. Forgiveness is the privilege of the person who has suffered the harm. So we must never ignore victims and their concerns – if a court appears lenient, it is not offering forgiveness, it is choosing a disposal which it hopes can be part of an offender's effective rehabilitation. And the reverse is true – if a victim chooses to forgive, perhaps recognising the potential for change in the offender, it is not for society to refuse them that opportunity.

A second thing to remember about forgiveness is that it can be a very slow and painful process for those who engage in it. Colin Firth and Nicole Kidman, in a new film, are playing the parts of my constituent Eric Lomax, who died last year, and his wife Patti. Eric was brutally tortured as a prisoner of the Japanese during World War II, and the film is based on his book The Railway Man. In it he describes just how long and painful the process was by which he was eventually able to offer forgiveness to one of his torturers, and how he gained a massive benefit and sense of release from it. His and other deeply moving accounts of the forgiveness journey, with its pain and its ultimately restorative power, reveal that forgiveness is not something to be talked about glibly, or presented as an easily applied technique in criminal justice policy.

It should come as no surprise to Christians that forgiveness is very difficult. That is why we prize so highly the forgiveness we see in the person of Jesus Christ. But for Christians and non-Christians alike, the concept of forgiveness, properly examined, offers insights into what we need to do with our criminal justice system. We need to be clear that, as well as public protection, our overcrowded prison system also serves as society's way of asserting what it will not tolerate; we have to find better and more effective ways of making that assertion while at the same time using sentences

But for Christians and non-Christians alike, the concept of forgiveness, properly examined, offers insights into what we need to do with our criminal justice system

which are more likely to reduce future offending. These may not all be custodial sentences. We should not be naive about criminal behaviour and the factors which contribute to it. A good start to this process may involve being honest with the public about the ineffectiveness of prison, rather than pandering to media headlines.

What Christians would not be justified in doing would be using our view of God's generosity in forgiveness as an argument that society should treat crime lightly, fail to challenge offenders over the wrong they have done, or presume to offer forgiveness on behalf of those who have suffered the effects of crime. Christian thinking tells us that people must be made to understand the consequences of their actions and the harm they have done. It should be an objective of the criminal justice process to make offenders face up to what they have done rather than allowing them to forget

> **It should be an objective of the criminal justice process to make offenders face up to what they have done rather than allowing them to forget about it or make excuses for it**

about it or make excuses for it. Christian thinking also tells us that forgiveness is a good thing, beneficial to both the forgiver and the forgiven. Although it is not the State's place to forgive on behalf of victims, it should be providing the opportunity for victims to extend forgiveness if they choose. In those cases where victims are able to engage with criminals in the application of restorative justice, there is the opportunity for both these objectives to be met and for the power of forgiveness to change lives.

6
Faith, Society and the State

Lord Tyler

My grandfather was a parish priest in Cornwall. When Parliament, comprising even then MPs of a wide variety of denominations, faiths and of none, refused to let the Church of England update the 1662 Prayer Book with a 1928 version, he declared himself converted to disestablishment.

The latest frustrating twist in the long tale of progress towards greater gender equality in the established church – the failure in November 2012 of a synod motion which would have made it lawful for women to be appointed as bishops – is just one manifestation of the totally confused relationship between faith and civil society in the UK today.

At its most trivial it is laughably anachronistic. When Archbishop Rowan Williams gave evidence to our Joint Committee of MPs and Peers on the reform of the Lords, I gently pointed out to him that the Bishops – from England alone – were only in Parliament ex officio as a hangover from their pre-Reformation medieval role as huge landowners and powerful fund managers on whom Monarchs depended when they went to war. He didn't demur. But when I asked whether, in his previous role, he, or the Church in Wales, or the Welsh nation as a whole felt deprived at the lack of representation in the Lords, he eventually replied ever so reasonably, "I am afraid that anachronism is, to me, a shortcut in an argument." But then he also spoke optimistically of fast-tracking women bishops into the Lords!

The whole of this discussion makes illuminating reading for anyone now concerned about the role of faith, and of the various religious institutions, in today's society.[1] Archbishop Williams was – and is – the most thoughtful and articulate analyst of these issues, and yet the overall impression left is that we live in a theological fog. If the established church was set up as a political artefact, to get round uncomfortable 16th Century royal matrimonial problems, why should not our 21st Century Parliament remove its exemption from gender equality laws?

If the established church was set up as a political artefact, to get round uncomfortable 16th Century royal matrimonial problems, why should not our 21st Century Parliament remove its exemption from gender equality laws?

There will be some who think that any dilution of the role of the Church of England would imply a deterioration of the whole country into further alienation from all faith, as well as a sign that we are retreating from our Christian heritage. Others, even practising Anglicans, would welcome a more realistic acknowledgement of the pattern of religious adherence in society today.

For example, the very limited state funding for the maintenance of church buildings, even the most precious architectural heritage of the cathedrals, is widely misunderstood and exaggerated in the public mind: they may think that the Government (i.e. the taxpayer) picks up the bill, and so resent making even a small contribution when they visit such buildings. By contrast, in France, where there is no national or established church, the state does indeed subsidise the upkeep of such national treasures, as a result of a dubious deal struck by Napoleon with the Catholic Church.

My impression is that members of other denominations, as well as of other faiths, are as confused as we Anglicans are. I have been told by prominent Muslims that they find the partial secularisation of our society, at all levels, much less easy to understand and respond to than they would in a more overtly Christian country. Others may well feel the same. However, we are where we are, as is so often said in other contexts. And I cannot see the clock retreating back to Victorian over-simplification, let alone to pre-Reformation church omnipotence.

My plea would be for more consistency and more transparency. Treat our fellow citizens as grown-ups, by acknowledging that we are now a multi-faith nation, with strong intra-faith links at all levels of society. If that means disestablishment for those of us who live in England, so be it. If that means that King Charles III decides to call himself "Defender of the Faiths", well why not?

I understand that since the Swedish Church was disestablished in 2001 it has gone from strength to strength, with new commitment to its mission and increasing membership. I have no reason to believe that the English sky would fall in, any more than it did in Wales.

Since the Swedish Church was disestablished in 2001 it has gone from strength to strength, with new commitment to its mission and increasing membership

Above all, I hope those of us who remain Anglicans can soon find a way to return to Christ's own teaching, and stop agonising over the dated views of my namesake Paul of Tarsus, let alone the washing up requirements of the Book of Leviticus. Sorting out a speedy way to implement the clear majority view of the Church that the "stained glass ceiling" for women priests is ludicrous, and offends all our Christian instincts, would be an excellent first step in this direction. Parliament, take note.

And if that in turn led on to a wider debate about the relationship between faith, society and the state, that would be an added bonus.

In the meantime this is, of course, not the only dilemma facing today's faith and civil opinion leaders. The apparent clash of equality legislation with religious freedom pops up in the most unexpected circumstances, as women, gay people, employers and legislators all bear witness. When does toleration of different religious and cultural traditions drift into acceptance of intolerance? Should we in turn differentiate between the basic original teaching of each other's faith on the one hand and the accumulated practice of subsequent generations on the other? And when should a liberal and democratic society intervene?

Professor Adam Dinham of the Faiths and Civil Society Unit is currently examining these issues with a wide cross-section of opinion leaders, under the auspices of the Equalities and Human Rights Commission. The background he identifies, both in recent UK and EU legislation, highlights, "Equality located as a central issue for social and human rights …. Only belatedly, in four pieces of legislation passed between 2000 and 2010, has religion been recognised and direct and indirect discrimination on religious grounds outlawed." Hence the urgent need for greater religious literacy at these levels of our national and local community.

Christians in politics, not least in Parliament, should enter this discussion confidently, not hiding behind outmoded and defensive dogmatic assertion

Christians in politics, not least in Parliament, should enter this discussion confidently, not hiding behind outmoded and defensive dogmatic assertion. If disestablishment assists our society and its institutions to come to terms with its multi-faith character, so be it. In particular, Anglicans who feel the need for the comfort blanket of the political invention of Henry VIII and Thomas Cromwell should read the award-winning historical novels of Hilary Mantel: if they still need that protective shell, then they might do well to examine the strength of their own faith!

Notes:
1 *Joint Committee on the Draft House of Lords Reform Bill evidence, 28 November 2011*

7
Am I my Brother's Keeper?

Lord Roberts of Llandudno

Six years ago I'd walked up to Trafalgar Square and noticed a number of young men on the grass bank outside the National Gallery. Some were clearly new arrivals in London, off a bus from another part of Europe, with fresh luggage and tidily dressed, possibly with dreams of new opportunities in London or elsewhere in the United Kingdom. Sharing the grass bank were others whose hopes had clearly been dashed and who looked as if the London experience had turned out to be more of a nightmare than a dream.

The immediate question was how to prevent the new arrivals from experiencing the defeat of those who shared the bank with them. How could we provide a safety net? This encouraged the formation of a co-ordinating group to bring together the various organisations tackling the problems of rough sleeping and homelessness. With the outstanding leadership of Dr George Gosling, who contacted the Salvation Army, Thames Reach, St Mungos, the Dallow Centre and various local authorities and other organisations, we met many times and were able to find ways of helping some of those in greatest need.

The problem of rough sleeping was particularly evident in the London area. If someone was homeless it was, and is, possible to provide food at different locations – although this can require those looking for help to travel some distance. There are extensive Clothing Centres and Shower facilities, but the main problem was, and is, finding safe places for sleeping. Beds were, and are, a problem.

Hostels, when accommodation is available, sometimes deter people because of problems such as drug taking, alcoholism and mental ill health. A large number of homeless people prefer to shelter in a shop doorway, a cardboard box or an underground passageway. Attempts to solve these kinds of problems continue and we owe a great debt to the wonderful people organising help.

BARKA is the name of a largely Polish 'help' foundation, which is inspirationally led by Ewa Sidowka whose parents in Poznan established the movement in late 1989. Thousands of needy people have been helped, either in the UK or by returning to Poland where farms, workshops, printing centres and even a purpose built holiday resort have enabled them to find their feet and resume a life of hope. It has been my privilege to co-operate with BARKA and witness their life-transforming work.

Early last December I crossed Oxford Street, London, through the Marble Arch Underground tunnel. In the tunnel were 20 or more absolutely destitute Romanians trying to rest on flattened cardboard boxes – this would be their overnight accommodation. These ranged from babes in arms to disabled and elderly people. The immediate follow up was a very positive Parliamentary meeting shared by the Metropolitan and Romanian police, the Romanian Embassy, Crisis and others. The conversations continue: what can we do to tackle poverty, cultural chasms and sometimes criminality? To what extent have we a responsibility towards them? Am I my brother's keeper?

> **The conversations continue: what can we do to tackle poverty, cultural chasms and sometimes criminality? To what extent have we a responsibility towards them? Am I my brother's keeper?**

The question, 'Am I my brother's keeper?' is asked by Cain who has killed his brother Abel. Cain and Abel were the sons of Adam and Eve. With the immense problems and needs surrounding us today, we ask ourselves this same question. To what extent do the actions of our society and we, ourselves, add to these problems? How can we, for instance, fulfil our obligation to asylum seekers, when political parties are making their situation more difficult?

In the Coalition we must make certain that our policies support the work being done, and that they in no way add to the problems which we are already trying to tackle. I hope very much that in the current Parliamentary session we can enhance our 'caring'

How can we, for instance, fulfil our obligation to asylum seekers, when political parties are making their situation more difficult?

reputation as liberals and Liberal Democrats, and that the manifesto for the 2015 General Election will bring hope and not despair to the most needy and vulnerable within our borders. This will call for very positive co-operation with other European nations: another good reason for maintaining our European vision.

8
Immigration: "...I was a stranger, and you took me in"

Baroness Brinton

"You shall not wrong a sojourner or oppress him, for you were sojourners in the land of Egypt." Exodus 22:21

When I was three, in 1958, we lived in Hong Kong, and I was aware of – but didn't understand the reason for – sudden arrivals of anxious people, bereft of any things. It was, of course, the beginning of the Great Leap Forward, and a lucky few managed to get out of China. Friends opened their hearts and their homes to these refugees without a second thought; even those who had very little of their own.

In Britain, we have had a long and proud history of helping those who come to our shores as sojourners, whether fleeing from oppression or seeking a better life in a country where they can make a real contribution.

> **Our modern world has become increasingly xenophobic, and it can be hard for the biblical voice to be heard**

In a Christian and liberal world, that would be enough. We all want to believe that a modern day Ruth, alone and bereft standing in the alien corn field, would have a Boaz to give more than the minimum duty necessary to support her. But our modern world has become increasingly xenophobic, and it can be hard for the biblical voice to be heard. How many of us have heard the shrill voice on the doorstep, complaining that all the best jobs are taken by immigrants, or that 'they' are getting free health services and welfare despite not contributing to the tax system?

Let's unpack 'sojourner'. I like this word in preference to 'stranger' which many Bible translations use. A sojourner is someone who arrives in a land, recognising that it isn't their natural home, and that they plan to be there on a temporary basis (however long temporary may be). Deuteronomy 10:18 tells us how we should treat them. "He executes justice for the fatherless and the widow, and loves the sojourner, giving him food and clothing".[2] We saw this love in practice when Citizens UK presented to our Federal Conference, to thank the Liberal Democrats for ending child detention in the UK. But of course, it is us who needed to thank them: offering that hand of friendship to the refugee and asylum seekers at a time when the tabloids screamed abuse, when xenophobic politicians from right and left attacked them, and when the state left them high and dry.

Here in Watford five years ago, Anna, a single mother with a young girl and twin toddlers fleeing religious persecution in Albania, was abandoned by her husband once they had arrived. Whilst waiting for their status to be assessed, they were asked to attend an interview in Liverpool – not Croydon, their nearest centre. If they failed to turn up, they would automatically lose their case. But without funds (Anna received only £30 per week child benefit), they couldn't even afford the train fare. Their local Watford and area refugee project not only provided the funds, but also a volunteer worker to accompany them, and provide sandwiches and drinks for the journey. Her presence was critical, for when Anna arrived with her children, the officer told them they had been written to in error and wanted to send them home. The volunteer demanded that the officer made the assessment after they had come so far, and he did, helping to speed up the decision to grant them asylum.

The funds for this journey, for the nappies and basic kitchen equipment that Anna received, and the specialist training for the volunteer, was provided by the churches in Watford and area, who see it as a part of their mission – mindful of Leviticus 19:33-4, "When a stranger sojourns with you in your land, you shall not do him wrong. You shall treat the stranger who sojourns with you as the native among you, and you shall love him as yourself, for you were strangers in the land of Egypt: I am the Lord your God."

But what about the economic migrant? It's easier to have sympathy with the sojourner who flees from oppression, but how do we respond to those who want to come here to better themselves? This is the sojourner that the BNP and UKIP and some tabloids want to see banned from our shores, alleging that they are taking scarce public resources.

We know that the reality is often different: migrant workers make a net contribution to our economy, and they are not entitled to services until they have paid their taxes. Answering the allegations of that frustrated resident, who believes that someone else is losing out because of migrants, takes some doing – and Liberal Democrats know better than most the impact of being honest about immigration at the last election! Yet we must continue to make that case. Xenophobia is more often about an easy target, rather than real threats. Once EU migration and international student numbers are removed, there are very few migrants coming here, and most have special skills that the UK needs.

It is good that Andrew Stunell is chairing a Liberal Democrat policy working party on immigration: we need new coherent policy. We cannot argue again for an amnesty for illegal immigrants; but are bonds for prospective immigrants and compulsory English language

> **I hope that we will not forget Hebrews 13:2: "Do not neglect to show hospitality to strangers, for thereby some have entertained angels unawares"**

lessons the appropriate successors? Whatever we vote for at the next party Conference, I hope that we will not forget Hebrews 13:2: "Do not neglect to show hospitality to strangers, for thereby some have entertained angels unawares."

Notes:

1 *Matthew 25:35, World English Bible*

2 *Deuteronomy 10:18, ESV. All other Bible references in this chapter are from the ESV unless otherwise stated.*

9
International Development and Nigeria

Mark Williams MP
MP for Ceredigion

If ever there was a justification for our Coalition Government's commitment to overseas aid, it was laid bare for me on a half-term trip to Nigeria as part of the All-Party Group on Global Education working with the charity ActionAid International in February 2012. I will never forget the village school in Abuja with 700 children with absolutely no water supply, no toilet provision, no drinking water, yet an abundance of enthusiastic youngsters; or the city school in Lagos proudly boasting its DFID-funded toilet block.

As a former teacher and as a Christian, I could not help but be struck by such sights. It reminded me of the reason why I had joined the teaching profession in the first place, and was a further reminder to me of our Christian duty (and joy) to help those less fortunate than ourselves. We have a responsibility as politicians to speak out against injustice and speak up for those who don't have a voice, even when it may not be popular, and that is a responsibility which I believe passes to all Christians of whatever denominational affiliation. I also believe that the best way to help people is to enable them to help themselves, and there is no more powerful method of ensuring this than the provision of good education. That was the vision behind the travelling schools of Griffith Jones in Wales almost three centuries ago, and the principle behind the first Sunday schools – education which was for everyone, no matter what their background or age.

> **We have a responsibility as politicians to speak out against injustice and speak up for those who don't have a voice, even when it may not be popular**

The case for education for all is not lost on the Nigerian Government Ministers I met. There are clear guidelines from the Federal Government, but aspirations are not cascading down in terms of adequate financial resources, and Nigeria is overwhelmed by the scale of the challenge: up to eight million out-of-school children, inadequate teacher training and a desperate school infrastructure. Add to this mix the differing policies in Nigeria's 36 states; the huge economic and cultural challenges where grinding poverty means parents can't release their kids for school; and, in the Islamic northern states in particular, the fact that girls are often discouraged from attending school. The DFID-funded Girls' Education Project is attempting to lessen the disparities between girls' and boys' enrolment in primary schools.[1]

> **Nigeria is overwhelmed by the scale of the challenge: up to eight million out-of-school children, inadequate teacher training and a desperate school infrastructure**

It is no surprise that the northern states are proving fertile territory for the terrorist group Boko Haren, as in these areas huge numbers are out of school and illiteracy levels are staggering. ActionAid and DFID through the Education Sector Support Programme in Nigeria are undertaking significant community empowerment work, promoting real community engagement through School-Based Management Committees.[2] It is hoped that engendering a sense of ownership for schools will actively promote the education sector. It was a pleasure to meet Civic Society leaders, parents, and traditional tribal and religious leaders actively demanding educational resources from their politicians.

There also remains the vexing issue of educational fees. Nigeria's Universal Basic Education Act of 2004 promotes free entitlement; however in reality even state schools are charging fees. Levied at perhaps only £2 a term, this is highly prohibitive to most families in a country where 64% live on less than a dollar a day. DFID has described Nigeria's educational system as facing "a multi-dimensional crisis". It is hampered by a wide perception of corruption at all levels of Government, and transparency and accountability have become key messages from Nigeria's commendably free Press. Nigeria is not an aid-dependent country. Indeed, aid represents less than 1% of GDP. The UK has a long history of involvement in Nigeria, and it is laudable that our support will help 800,000 more children into education in Nigeria, including 600,000 girls, and encourage 5,000 women in rural areas from the north into teacher training. The need is there; the opportunities are vast.

I have focussed on Nigeria because of the personal connection I have with that country as a result of my trip there last year, but the same needs and the same opportunities are mirrored across the developing world. The commendable work which has been carried out by a myriad of charities in this sector continues and is to be encouraged: whether it is Tearfund getting children back into the classroom in Haiti, well after the impact of the earthquake there has left our news screens; or Wycliffe Bible Translators teaching literacy, helping to grow local cultures and educating people in their native language. Of course the work is by no means limited to charities with an overtly Christian ethos. There are many like ActionAid International, with whom I went to Nigeria, that are working just as hard to improve literacy and educate children and adults across the world, so they can better their prospects. They are helping to provide communities, and indeed whole countries, with the skills to improve their economic prospects and at the same time giving hope to children in those countries who aspire to a better future.

As an MP I have an opportunity, far greater than many, to change the future of these communities: to highlight the need and work to ensure that it is met. I also have the ability to speak out on behalf of these communities across the world, in the House of Commons and more widely – something I have taken advantage of in the past. I believe passionately in the power of good education that is available for all and free to access. As I have explained, this passion is rooted in a Christian

This passion is rooted in a Christian belief that we have a responsibility to share what we have been given

belief that we have a responsibility to share what we have been given, and to provide the means by which people with little hope can reach their true potential – and inspire others to do the same.

Notes:

1 http://projects.dfid.gov.uk/project.aspx?Project=104199
2 http://projects.dfid.gov.uk/project.aspx?Project=104200

10
It's Good to be Green

Duncan Hames MP
MP for Chippenham

To be someone with a concern for our environment you don't have to be a Christian, or a liberal, but many people – myself included – are all three, and I'd argue that isn't simply a coincidence.

That Liberal Democrats take the environment seriously in our campaigning and policy development seems hardly in need of saying to most readers of this book. To the uninitiated, however, a simple glance at the numerous green tags on policies when flicking through our manifesto for the last general election gives a clear indication of how thinking of the environment and sustainability, permeates our policy platform. Our campaign in that election cast us as "the only party in British politics that can and will put the environment at the heart of government".[1] Since then, we have proven it to be so, advancing in the Coalition the Green Investment Bank, the Green Deal home insulation scheme, and the commitment to an 80% cut in greenhouse gas emissions by 2050. Furthermore our commitment to the Green Climate Fund, and this year delivering on the promise to the world's poorest people of 0.7% of gross national income in international aid, show that we recognise the need to help those most severely affected by climate change.

That Christians have cause to be similarly green is increasingly widely observed in practice, but perhaps less well established in theory. So I think it is worth making the case for it here.

More interesting, I would contend, is the convergence in the motivations of liberals and Christians behind this common cause. There is increasing recognition of the importance of environmental conditions for the fulfilment of any quality of human life, as well as for the health and diversity of nature itself. People are beginning to appreciate that gases emitted from factories and power stations in Britain ultimately impact on the ability of smallholder farmers to feed their communities in Africa and elsewhere. As environmental and humanitarian instincts align, questions of environmental policy reveal more and more about our attitudes to social justice around the world. Some Christians may not have found themselves moved by conservationist calls on behalf of plants and pandas, but surely this broader concern demands a response?

Yet all three: liberals, environmentalists, and Christians, feel the pressure of these tough economic times - where natural human instincts of scapegoating, self-preservation, and fear loom large – and not for the first time. In June 2007, 13% of Britons said the environment was one of the most important issues facing the country; now just 5% do, according to the polling firm Ipsos MORI.[2]

> **So I will argue that we should embrace this shared concern and make a practice of working together: Christians should demand green policies from their politicians, and Liberal Democrats should engage with churches**

So I will argue that we should embrace this shared concern and make a practice of working together: Christians should demand green policies from their politicians, and Liberal Democrats should engage with churches involved in campaigns such as Fairtrade, Enough Food IF and Make Poverty History and the Jubilee 2000 Coalition before them. In my own experience it has been a welcome context for sharing both my faith and my politics. By building big coalitions across civil society, these campaigns make a vital difference to the lives of people around the world.

Attitudes to the environment in the Church

Commitment to environmentalism is now widespread across the denominational and geographical divide. Solar panels line many of the buildings in the Vatican City, a result of the Apostolic See's commitment to become a carbon-neutral state.[3] In 2005, the Anglican Communion Environmental Network declared that, "Willfully causing environmental degradation is a sin".[4] Closer to home, the Church of England is committed to reducing the carbon footprint of its buildings by 42% by 2020, and by 80% by 2050.[5] American evangelical Christians' reputation for a supposed 'end of days' indifference to environmental woes is belied by organisations such as the Evangelical Environmental Network, which was founded in America in 1993 to explore "the Bible's teaching on the responsibility of God's people to 'tend the garden' through a faithful walk with our Lord Jesus Christ".[6]

Of course we cannot ignore the way some conservative evangelicals continue to dispute any theological justification for environmentalism. The Cornwall Group hopes to slay "the Green Dragon", which spokesman Dr E. Calvin Beisner sees as "an alternative world view and a substitute for Christianity".[7] James Watt, US Secretary of the Interior under Ronald Reagan, argued in 1982 that "the earth was put here by the Lord for His people to subdue and use for profitable purposes on their way to the hereafter".[8] This line of thinking must encourage the critique of Lynn White Jr, who argued in 1967 that the Judaeo-Christian tradition caused the ecological crisis by teaching that "no item in the physical creation had any purpose save to serve man's purposes".[9] The biblical basis for his view is provided by the 'Dominion Mandate', which is found in Genesis 1:28:

"And God blessed them [Adam and Eve]. And God said to them, 'Be fruitful and multiply and fill the earth and subdue it, and have dominion over the fish of the sea and over the birds of the heavens and over every living thing that moves on the earth.'"

But to me, and I'm sure to most Christians, "dominion" in this passage should be interpreted as responsible stewardship rather than exploitative tyranny.[10] Further evidence of man's duty to protect the earth abounds throughout the Bible, from God's order to Adam and Eve to work and keep the garden[11] to the instruction in Leviticus that "you shall not strip your vineyard bare",[12] to Jesus's observation of the Father's care for even the smallest sparrow.[13] But I am aware that selective quoting is only so persuasive.

Christian support for environmentalism is also driven by concern for the world's dispossessed, in the spirit of Jesus' lesson that, "as you did it to one of the least of these my brothers, you did it to me".[14] This demands a more urgent response, both on a liberal basis – to prevent harm – and a Christian one. Archbishop Desmond Tutu is compelling when he writes that, "the poor and the vulnerable are members of God's family and are the most severely affected by droughts, high temperatures, the flooding of coastal cities, and more severe and unpredictable weather events resulting from climate change".[15]

Rowan Williams, when Archbishop of Canterbury, made an even more urgent case. He argued that environmental crisis does not simply lead to "spiralling poverty and mortality", but also "brutal and uncontainable conflict", as competition for scarce resources breaks out into violence.[16]

Christian campaigning and action for the environment

Having established a theological case for environmental concern, we must turn it into action. The role of Christians in this respect is extensive. A 2007 survey by the UK Environment Agency asked leading British environmentalists for "50 things that will save the planet".[17] Number two on their list was that religious leaders make the planet their priority.

In the secular political world, international co-operation is key to responding to assaults on our environment. So it is among churches. Indeed, this is where Christian communities possess a distinct advantage. They have much experience of bridging national borders, and denominational ones too. The European Christian Environmental Network (ECEN) was founded in 1997 to encourage its members to act on churches' ecological responsibilities. It is a genuinely ecumenical organisation, which co-operates with the World Council of Churches and with the European Catholic Bishops' Conference. Its last assembly, in the Dutch town of Elspeet in the Netherlands, saw participants (including a member of the UN Committee on Development Policy) from over 20 countries meet to discuss the "tensions between a culture demanding infinite economic growth that is dependent on a planet with finite resources", and to assess how these might be overcome.[18]

Furthermore, some organisations are known for their focus on practical action. Christian Aid is primarily driven by a desire to tackle poverty and injustice. It has realised that preventing the worst of climate change and mitigating its impact is a crucial way in which to do this. In Malawi, Christian Aid has installed solar panels to generate electricity. This has enabled many villages to benefit from power for the first time. In Senegal, a partner of Christian Aid is training local people to use energy-efficient stoves, which require far less fuel than conventional cooking methods.[19] Christian Aid does not only hope to address the direct impact of climate change; it also works to tackle its causes. Its primary motivation for this is the injustice that sees Western countries emit the most carbon per head while the developing world suffers the gravest consequences. The organisation has worked on developing compensation schemes to benefit poor countries, as well as ensuring that carbon emissions are brought down in the developed world.

A Rocha is another Christian organisation that combines a commitment to biodiversity with a passion for lifting people out of poverty.[20] In West London it has co-operated with the London Borough of Hillingdon to transform a 90-acre derelict site, previously known as the Minet tip, in the midst of a high-density urban area, into Minet Country Park - which has since been awarded the Green Flag Award, a benchmark national standard for parks and green spaces in the UK. This is a telling reminder that people can suffer from environmental degradation close to home too. A Rocha also takes a global perspective. Its Ugandan branch has been assisting people living in shanty towns around Kampala, whose homes are perched on the edge of Lubigi Wetland – one of the largest marshy areas near the capital. The organisation has improved sanitation and provided clean drinking water for the local community while campaigning for the protection of wildlife in the wetlands area.

Tearfund has done similarly laudable work in helping the victims of climate change, in places ranging from the Monze East area of Zambia to Rajasthan in India.[21] It has also done important work in engaging with policy makers. Its representatives attended the UN Framework Convention on Climate Change conference in Nairobi in 2006. Alongside many other Christian organisations such as Christian

Aid, Cafod, The Salvation Army, and the Church of England, it is a supporter of the 'Enough Food IF' campaign, which aims to bring an end to world hunger, and whose efforts I have promoted in Parliament.

There is also a place for organisations which spread an environmental message within religious bodies. An organisation called Eco-Congregation acts in England, Scotland, Wales and Ireland, encouraging churches to carry out an environmental check-up. The John Ray Initiative, a UK educational charity, was formed to bring together scientific and Christian understandings of the environment, and to communicate them in an easily-understandable way. It helps run educational courses on the environment, such as the Certificate in Christian Rural and Environmental Studies course at Ripon College, near Oxford.

Let's work together

I hope I have shown how Jesus' appeal to "love your neighbour as yourself"[22] has clear implications for any Christian's approach to the environment. The work being done by a wide array of organisations, from Christian Aid to Tearfund and many more, demonstrate that this belief can drive action across the world, and lead to crucial co-operation between both secular groups and religious ones. The Liberal Democrats should work with them to make our vision of a sustainable future a reality.

> **Jesus' appeal to "love your neighbour as yourself" has clear implications for any Christian's approach to the environment**

Environmental action is a good work that Liberal Democrats and Christians, as well as Christians who are Liberal Democrats should all embrace.

Reflecting on hustings organised by churches at election time, I'm struck that, while they are a welcome contribution to our democratic process, so many people there feel uncomfortable. How many of the questions can be Christian? When should the candidates reveal their faith, lack of, or rejection of it? How authentic are the answers they give? I'm not convinced that responses to questions on stereotypical

'Christian' issues get anywhere near telling the full story of who we are. Like many Christians, my faith drives my commitment to championing the environment and sustainable development in a fairer world. Perhaps, as I have tried to show here, by campaigning on the environment, and on behalf of the poorest people in the world, Christians and Liberal Democrats alike can be better understood.

Notes:

1 *Liberal Democrat Manifesto 2010 http://network.libdems.org.uk/manifesto2010/libdem_manifesto_2010.pdf*

2 *Ipsos MORI Issues Index, 20 Jun 2013, p14 http://www.ipsos-mori.com/Assets/Docs/Polls/June13IssuesIndexslides.pdf*

3 *E Rosenthal, New York Times, 'Vatican seeks to be carbon neutral', 3 Sep 2007 http://www.nytimes.com/2007/09/03/business/worldbusiness/03iht-carbon.4.7366547.html?pagewanted=all&_r=0*

4 *Statement to The Anglican Communion from The Anglican Communion Environmental Network, Apr 2005 http://www.melbourne.anglican.com.au/NewsAndViews/Issues/environment/Documents/Anglican%20Communion%20Network%20Statement.pdf*

5 *The Church of England, Shrinking the Footprint campaign http://www.churchofengland.org/about-us/our-buildings/shrinking-the-footprint.aspx*

6 *As stated on their website: http://www.creationcare.org*

7 *L Hickman, The Guardian, 'The US evangelicals who believe environmentalism is a 'native evil'', 5 May 2011 http://www.guardian.co.uk/environment/blog/2011/may/05/evangelical-christian-environmentalism-green-dragon*

8 *J Watt, Saturday Evening Post 'Ours is the Earth', Jan/Feb 1982, pp74-75, quoted in J Foster, The Ecology of John Calvin, 18 Dec 2005, p16 http://myseminary.org/articles/jas_foster/pt.jas_foster.calvin.ecology.pdf*

9 *L White Jr, Science, 'The Historical Roots of Our Ecological Crisis', Vol 155, No 3767, Mar 1967, p1205 http://www.drexel.edu/~/media/Files/greatworks/pdf_fall09/HistoricalRoots_of_EcologicalCrisis.ashx*

10 *As Pope Benedict XVI has said: "The true meaning of God's original command, as the Book of Genesis clearly shows, was not a simple conferral of authority, but rather a summons to responsibility." (Message for the celebration of the World Day of Peace, 1 Jan 2010 http://www.vatican.va/holy_father/benedict_xvi/messages/peace/documents/hf_ben-xvi_mes_20091208_xliii-world-day-peace_en.html)*

11 *Genesis 2:15, ESV*

12 *Leviticus 19:10, ESV*

13 *Matthew 10:29, ESV*

14 *Matthew 25:40, ESV*

15 *D Tutu, Foreword to The Green Bible (Harper Bibles), p1-13*

16 *Dr R Williams, Ecology and Economy speech at the University of Kent, 8 Mar 2005 http://rowanwilliams.archbishopofcanterbury.org/articles.php/1550/ecology-and-economy-archbishop-calls-for-action-on-environment-to-head-off-social-crisis*

17 *'The 50 things that will save the planet' in Environment Agency, Your Environment, Issue 17, Nov 2007 to Jan 2008 http://image.guardian.co.uk/sys-files/Environment/documents/2007/10/31/50top.pdf*

18 *Christian Ecology Link, European Christian Environmental Network (ECEN) Aug 2012 Elspeet, Netherlands, 5 Sep 2012 http://www.greenchristian.org.uk/archives/3452*

19 *Christian Aid, Energy Saving Stove http://www.flickr.com/photos/christianaidimages/5613004485*

20 *http://www.arocha.org/gb-en/index.html*

21 *Tearfund & Institute of Development Studies, Adapting to climate change, 2006 http://www.tearfund.org/webdocs/website/Campaigning/policy%20and%20research/Adapting%20to%20climate%20change%20discussion%20paper.pdf*

22 *Mark 12:31, ESV*

11
Liberal language and the Christian calling

Sarah Teather MP
MP for Brent Central

Liberal /ˈlɪb(ə)r(ə)l/ 1. a. given, or giving freely, generous, not sparing of, abundant.

It is an old definition from a dog-eared yellow-paged Oxford English dictionary I have had since I was a teenager.[1] More modern editions begin with politics and theology, before consigning the adjective to over-consumption (he poured himself a liberal helping of wine). An inauspicious start perhaps in an era of austerity.

But the old use of the word has always captured something of my sense of the party – something more spiritual than literal. Something in our attitude to people.

Liberalism, it seems to me, is an optimistic and hopeful creed. It thinks well of people. It trusts them with power. It values their contribution. It seeks their views. It develops their talents. It encourages creativity.

It has a generous spirit.

There is a need for that generosity of spirit in political discourse today. On benefits, on poverty, on immigration, the public mood is angry and resentful. Restricted by collective responsibility, hampered by austerity, conscious of the strength of public opinion and fearful of the next election, Liberal Democrats have watched and winced at others' mean characterisations and occasionally indulged in a few of our own. But mostly, we have been uncomfortably silent.

In the absence of our witness, it has been left to Christian churches to provide an alternative narrative.

As I write, we are now less than two years from a General Election. All the indications are that austerity will continue for some time. Families will feel the strain for longer than we could ever have feared. Against that backdrop of anxiety, messages that find an easy enemy to blame for our woes, be they immigrants or welfare claimants, are likely to find fertile ground. As a party, we need to decide how to respond. We stand at a crossroads.

I want to suggest here that the alternative narrative, articulated by many Christian churches over the last few months, may help us find our way. Christianity brings a rather different anthropology: a different view of what it means to be human and on what is valuable. It has some pretty challenging things to say to politics at the moment. But I think those challenges are likely to resonate particularly with Liberal Democrats, even those without faith, many of whom are uneasy about the same kind of things and have been struggling to find the words to articulate the problem they see.

Let me begin with an epithet that captures much of what I am referring to.

When George Osborne stepped into the public outcry against Mick Philpott, just before Philpott was sentenced to jail for the killing of his six children in April 2013,[2] Osborne knew full well that he would cause a row. His comments about the state 'subsidising' lifestyles such as Philpott's, was a deliberate and calculated attempt to draw all benefit claimants into the devastating wreckage of one man's selfishness. And yet, the media coverage was all of a type, and in this regard, it illustrated perfectly the nature of the discourse which is so deeply ingrained in Westminster politics.

No one asked in the storm that followed whether Osborne's analysis was correct, true, honest, or helpful. No one stopped to wonder whether his words would have any impact on the lives of those he included. Instead, the analysis all focused on tactics. Was it an astute reading of public mood or had he over-reached himself? Did he wrong-foot opponents, or would it backfire?

Labour meanwhile launched an excoriating attack on his remarks, on grounds of taste, only to undermine that three days later when their Deputy Leader responded to reactive poll anxieties by declaring that hard working families are exasperated with large poor families.[3] It seems demonising others is only a problem when nasty people do it.

Osborne's interjection was very much in keeping with other colourful characterisations of those on welfare. It was also in keeping with an approach to policy making which has spawned headline-grabbing popular proposals (like the universal household benefit cap for example), which will have a devastating impact on some families[4] (the kind who have traditionally low voting rates), and yield no positive outcome for society as a whole. The prime motive of such interventions is to create a political device to make clear whose side you are on (the skivers or the strivers), not actually to affect unemployment, or to save money, or indeed to make money, create jobs, or work towards any bigger vision of a better society. The energising desire is just that of riding a short term wave of anger from anxious voters against those who appear to be escaping from the consequences of the current crisis scot-free.

There are clear moral issues at stake with such a divisive approach. Instrumentalising and then demonising successive groups of people for short term poll gain is born of a politics that has forgotten any notion of public service.

But this is as nothing in comparison with the rush to follow polling leads on immigration, which looks set to dominate political discourse for at least the next 12 months. Just before Easter 2013, all parties, our own included, indulged in a bit of this fail-safe enemy baiting. Many sabres were rattled across the three week period in which the three party political leaders made their pitches.[5] The combined effect of all speeches on public mood and attention was more than the sum of its parts. This culmination of this three week period coincided in the Christian calendar with the start of Holy Week, when congregations listen to the long Gospel reading of the Passion,[6] and are given bit-parts in the role play as a member of the baying mob. Pilate's placating of the crowd held a particular sharpness that weekend.

There is sometimes a view inside the Westminster bubble that, ultimately, it is only the detail of policy and legislation that matter. Spin, argument, press coverage, speeches: that is all just a means to an end. I cannot understand how anyone who has actually served as a Government Minister and given any careful reflection to the conversations they have with people whose lives they touch can go on believing that.

What politicians say matters. It matters in far more profound ways than just blips in opinion polls

What politicians say matters. It matters in far more profound ways than just blips in opinion polls. People make decisions about their lives, consciously and unconsciously, as a result of the things that we say and the arguments that we make and the way that they are then reported. If you remain unconvinced, think about the panic that erupted when a fuel tanker strike threatened, and the disastrous consequences that followed a minor remark by a Cabinet Minister about the benefits of jerry cans.[7]

In a world where speeches and press stories are merely the means to an end, you will often hear an argument that runs a little like this: "if we don't make the argument on immigration it will be taken over by those who have truly awful intentions". Or, "we cannot ignore public opinion here; unless we shore up confidence in the welfare system we will lose it altogether". Now there may be elements of fact in both of those statements. But it fails to take responsibility for the contribution we ourselves make to the problem we claim to be trying to remedy.

The demonising of welfare claimants and immigrants has a tangible impact on real lives as they are lived and experienced. It has a profound impact on the subjects of the characterisation as they are rejected from full participation in society. But it also leaves wider legacies for society as a whole. It affects how neighbours rub up against one another. The way children make friends in the playground. The decisions and choices adults make about where to live, how to live, where to work, whether to claim benefits they are entitled to. The friendships that all of us form. The charities that we donate to. How we respond to strangers. The respect afforded to individuals by agents of the state. And then in turn, the press coverage which is given. And the policies which are made in response to that. And the speeches which are given. And the cycle begins again.

Whether you think any of this matters rather depends on how you view the world, what motivates you, what kind of society you would like to see flourish. It also depends on the extent to which you are aware of a politician's relationship with the citizens they serve, of citizens' relationships with others, and the extent to which these relationships are dynamic and generative. And most importantly, what value and purpose you ascribe to those relationships.

Christian leaders have consistently criticised the demonisation of immigrants[8] and welfare claimants[9] because Christianity has a very particular view about what it means to be human, about human value and worth. A worth that transcends notions of wealth or popularity, of acceptable behaviour or conduct, of race or creed or country of birth. Christianity professes that all are precious and worthy of dignity, as beings created in the image of a loving God.[10]

> **Christian leaders have consistently criticised the demonisation of immigrants and welfare claimants because Christianity has a very particular view about what it means to be human, about human value and worth**

This – that we are made in God's own image and bear his imprint – is core to understanding Christian anthropology. It is the reason Christians concern themselves with the well-being of others, and it grounds our hope in human nature: if all are made in the image of a loving, creative, good and generous God, all people have the potential to be likewise.

Christianity also says something else about human beings: that we are at heart relational creatures – defined by our interpersonal relationships, with God and with one another.[11] Christianity's very notion of God is relational. We profess a three-personed God, Father, Son and Holy Spirit, each distinct and yet united, existing in perfect relationship with one another. A relationship into which God draws us in a model of perfect communion, "that they may be one even as we are one".[12]

More than this, Catholic Christians hold to a sacramental vision of the world. That is to say that they believe the world around them to be a place where they can meet, touch and encounter God and respond to Him. All is gift;[13] indeed the whole world is "charged with the grandeur of God".[14]

Christianity, and indeed the Jewish tradition on which it is founded, consistently asks us to give particular attention to the most vulnerable members of society.[15] We are asked to seek and find the face of Christ in the poor, the hungry, the sick, the imprisoned and the stranger and to serve those as we would our Lord.[16] Catholic social teaching on the need for a preferential option for the poor is rooted in this idea of Jesus identifying himself with the least amongst people.[17]

But in all, we are reminded that we are interdependent. The well-being of one impacts upon the well-being of another. The common good is a concern to us all, because it affects us all and indeed belongs to us all. But we cannot promote the common good just by improving the average level of well-being, or even getting the greatest benefit for the greatest number of people. Averages and additions don't work when people are interdependent. It is much more like "a multiplication sum, where if any one number is zero then the total is always zero. If anyone is left out and deprived of what is essential then the common good has been betrayed."[18]

If the world around you is a place where you encounter the Divine, and if you look for Christ especially in the face of the poorest, what follows logically from that is a perspective on policy-making which is inclusive and not exclusive. One that is concerned to foster the conditions in communities that enable trusting, flourishing human relationships to develop. That extends a special care to those who are most vulnerable, even in the face of others' hostility. That is prepared to speak against the heaping of abuse onto those at the bottom of the hierarchy of public opinion, be they asylum seekers or benefit claimants, not just to safeguard their dignity, but also because such dehumanising behaviour ultimately infects us all.

Christianity has a full and clear narrative to explain why we should protect the most vulnerable even when unpopular. But I think this fact of our common humanity is something most instinctively know to be true. Perhaps this is the "persuasive echo in the heart of every person",[19] but certainly many an unbeliever has oft quoted and understood the poem by Lutheran Pastor Martin Niemöller, First they came for the communists.[20]

Christianity, however, makes rather greater demands on us than just to refrain from being nasty to one another. It calls on us to relate to one another as God relates to us. To love as we have been loved,[21] and to model our relationships with one another in our families and communities on this basis.

How have we been loved? The Old and the New Testaments are full of rich images of this love and care. The Psalmist's song of thanksgiving to God says, "You care for the earth, give it water, you fill it with riches. Your river in heaven brims over to provide its grain."[22] "...you anoint me with the purest oil."[23] And elsewhere, "He kept him as the apple of his eye."[24] And in lavish imagery Isaiah says, "You shall be a crown of beauty in the hand of the Lord, and a royal diadem in the hand of your God."[25] Jesus promises to those who give, that "it will be given to you. A good measure, pressed down, shaken together, running over, will be put into your lap..."[26] And of God, "...I am generous".[27] And of himself, "I came that they may have life, and have it abundantly."[28]

It is an image of love given freely, generously, not sparing, given abundantly.

Christianity, it seems to me, is a hopeful creed. It speaks of a God who sees us as we are, and yet loves us and believes in us all the same. A God who trusts us with freedom. Who values our contribution. Who cares for our views. Who develops our talents. Who encourages creativity.

A God who is the Spirit of generosity.

This is a God who loves liberally. And Christianity calls on us to do the same.

> **Christianity, with its clear teaching on the value of each human being, of the dignity they should be afforded, of the worth that is gifted, undiminished by changes in opinion polls or fashion or political whim, has an authority to speak by virtue of its consistency**

I believe that Christian Liberal Democrats have a particular contribution to make as we, both as a party and a wider political community, stand at this crossroad and deliberate on the best way forward. Christianity, with its clear teaching on the value of each human being, of the dignity they should be afforded, of the worth that is gifted, undiminished by changes in opinion polls or fashion or political whim, has an authority to speak by virtue of its consistency. Christianity brings with it an understanding of human nature which values and cherishes relationship. It can speak to the hidden anxieties in communities, to the deeper concerns that lie beneath the surface noise about immigration and poverty. It hears the deeper need in the fear of stranger and of other but it calls on us to reach out, and extend a welcome.

Liberal Democrats have always stood shoulder to shoulder with the weakest. Our belief in the inalienable rights of each individual human being has allowed us to swim against the tide of popular opinion and defend their cause. Our very name tells the story of the tensions we hold in balance: liberalism is there to temper the risk of a tyranny of the majority empowered by democracy. If we do not defend the most vulnerable members of society when popular opinion turns, no one else in politics will.

Christianity calls on Liberal Democrats to hold sure to the generosity of spirit that is in our liberal name. It calls us to be hopeful. To be generous. To value people. All people. To seek their contribution. To develop their talents. To foster their creativity.

Christianity calls on liberals to be true to who we really are. That is a vocation only we can fulfil. And the question I ask is this: is there really anyone else we would rather be?

Notes:

1 *The Oxford Dictionary of Current English, edited by RE Allen, reprinted 1990, OUP*

2 *Mick Philpott case: 'George Osborne benefit comments spark row', BBC newsonline, 5 April 2013*

3 *'Working parents exasperated over large families on benefits says Harman', Guardian, 7 April 2013*

4 *Impact assessment for Household Benefit Cap; published by DWP, 2011*

5 *Ed Miliband, Labour Party political broadcast, 6 March 2013; Nick Clegg, speech on immigration, London, 22 March 2013; David Cameron, speech on immigration and welfare, University Campus, Suffolk, 25 March 2013.*

6 *Gospel reading for Palm Sunday, Luke 22:14–23:56.*

7 *'Francis Maude urged to quit over petrol panic as union rules out Easter strike', Guardian, 30 March 2012.*

8 *Choosing the common good, Catholic Bishops' Conference of England and Wales, 2010, p15.*

9 *The blame game must stop, Church Action on Poverty, 2013; The lies we tell ourselves, A report from the Baptist Union of Great Britain, the Methodist Church, the Church of Scotland and the United Reformed Church, 2013.*

10 *This is the doctrine of imago Dei, which is based on Gen 1:26–27 and its interpretation.*

11 *Benedict XVI, Caritas in Veritate, Sec 53, 2009.*

12 *John 17:22, RSV.*

13 *James 1:17, NRSV.*

14 *The Grandeur of God, in Poems, Gerald Manley Hopkins, 1918.*

15 *As indeed does Islam, but that and similar calls made by other religions on its followers is a subject for a different publication.*

16 *Matthew 25:34–40, NRSV.*

17 *John Paul II, Sollicitudo Rei Socialis, Sec 43, 1987.*

18 *Op cit. 8, p8.*

19 *John Paul II, Evangelium vitae, Sec 2, 1995.*

20 *„Als die Nazis die Kommunisten holten...", Martin Niemöller, 1946.*

21 *John 13:34, NRSV.*

22 *Psalm 64(65):9, Breviary.*

23 *Psalm 91(92):10, Breviary.*

24 *Deut 32:10, Breviary.*

25 *Is 62:3, Breviary.*

26 *Luke 6:38, NRSV.*

27 *Matthew 20:15, NRSV.*

28 *John 10:10, NRSV.*

21343378R00052

Made in the USA
Charleston, SC
16 August 2013